"This book is so much more than a workbook! While capturing the key parts of Jay Earley's *Self-Therapy* in a workbook format, it also elucidates IFS best practices and will be indispensable to IFS students, teachers, clients, coaches, and therapists."

—Everett Considine, IFS Instructor and Certified IFS Practitioner

"*Self-Therapy Workbook* by Bonnie Weiss, LCSW, is a comprehensive, thoughtful and well organized accompaniment for anyone working to build the capacities of self-leadership. The workbook is an exemplary introduction to the IFS Model for first timers, yet it also brings enough sophistication in detail and scope to benefit professional-level providers. As usual, Ms. Weiss brings a collection of excellent meditations to open the reader's inner experience as well as plenty of room to record one's own reflections and progressive growth. I highly recommend this workbook for individuals and professions as a valuable enhancement to the therapeutic process."

—Roseanne Keefe, LICSW

"If you want an easy way to understand and effectively utilize the IFS process, this workbook clearly breaks down the steps described in *Self-Therapy* by Jay Earley. The exercises are clear, the images are helpful and well integrated into the text, and the examples make this workbook easy to use. I appreciate that it has expanded the original work to include chapters on polarization and couples work. I will certainly give this to my clients to both educate them about the IFS process and to empower them to use this process on their own."

—Nancy Dagenhart, MFT, IFS Therapist

"This workbook is a very useful companion to *Self-Therapy*. It provides thoughtful step-by-step guidance through the IFS process. Its clarity and simplicity allow the reader to turn the theoretical concepts of IFS into practical, useful steps toward healing. A must-read for those who want to use IFS for self-growth and healing."

—Ilyssa Bass, IFS Therapist, Jerusalem, Israel

"This book is a gold mine. It takes the excellent *Self-Therapy* book to the next level in terms of practicality. I'm convinced that this workbook will help its readers process and work through inner blocks and recurring pains. It is a reference I will use personally as well as recommend to my clients."

—Ronnie Grandell, Psychologist, Finland

Self-Therapy Workbook

An Exercise Book for the IFS Process

Bonnie J. Weiss, LCSW

⬚ PATTERN SYSTEM BOOKS

Larkspur, CA

▧ PATTERN SYSTEM BOOKS

140 Marina Vista Ave.
Larkspur, CA 94939
415-924-5256
www.patternsystembooks.com

ISBN: 978-0-9843927-4-2

Printed in the United States of America

ACKNOWLEDGMENTS

I primarily want to thank Jay Earley for his generosity in allowing me to use his material as a basis for this book. I appreciate his support for this vision and his tireless commitment to bringing the healing concepts of IFS to the larger public.

It was great fun spending a weekend writing the couples chapter with my dear friend Marla Silverman. Any time with Marla is treasured time well spent. We always depend on Kira Freed for editing and, in this case, design. We love her sharp eye, open heart, and clear language. Thank you for always making time for our projects.

I deeply appreciate Alexis Zielke's creative input and loving support on this project. I so value her fresh point of view. As usual, Jeanenne Chase Langford and MJ Stern are always there to pick up pieces and move things along. I am grateful for their support. Thanks again to Karen Donnelly for the use of her illustrations. I have always valued the way they make the concepts come alive.

TABLE OF CONTENTS

LIST OF EXERCISES

INTRODUCTION

This workbook is a companion book to *Self-Therapy* by Jay Earley, PhD. *Self Therapy* lays out the step-by-step process of the Internal Family Systems Therapy Model originated by Richard Schwartz, PhD (www.selfleadership.org). The book is designed to facilitate learning the basics of the IFS process. The workbook takes you step-by-step from accessing a part by working with Protectors through getting to know and heal the more fragile, exiled parts of the psyche. The format of integrated concept descriptions and exercises is ideal for individual exploration, small groups, or classes. Exercises can be done on one's own or with a partner. The workbook structure allows for journal-style following of your process.

The workbook provides summaries of the steps outlined by Earley and offers expanded exercises to work with and integrate the IFS process. Sample responses to the exercises are provided in order to clarify the ideas being explored. The workbook goes beyond *Self-Therapy* by including chapters on using IFS with couples, polarization, and firefighters. For a fuller explanation of various IFS ideas, transcripts of sessions and case examples refer to *Self-Therapy*.

As clinicians, Jay and I were very excited to discover the IFS Model. It allowed us to integrate our training and clinical experience with our years of spiritual practice. The concept of Self brings into the therapeutic arena the power of higher consciousness as a healing tool. We are deeply grateful to Dick Schwartz for his unflagging commitment to bring this model into the world.

Over the years of teaching the IFS Model and using it with clients, Jay and I have provided user-friendly materials that enable people to use the powerful tools of IFS in their individual efforts to grow and develop their humanness as well as to transform personal difficulties. Being psychotherapists, we deeply value the importance of the helping relationship and the sacredness of the therapeutic encounter. We do, however, believe that people can benefit from being introduced to this model outside of therapy and can work by themselves or with a partner to further their personal understanding and gain some relief from internal structures that have limited their ability to function in a satisfying way. Our hope is that this workbook will supplement existing material by providing a clear, easy-to-follow structure for doing IFS work.

Downloadable exercise pages that accompany this workbook are available at http://personal-growth-programs.com/self-therapy-workbook-bonnie-weiss/

Chapter 1

BASIC IFS CONCEPTS

Internal Family Systems (IFS) is a relatively new form of therapy that is compassionate, inclusive, spiritual, powerfully healing, and deeply respectful of our inner life. IFS recognizes that our psyches are made up of different parts, sometimes called subpersonalities. You can think of them as little people inside us. Each part has its own perspective, feelings, memories, goals, and motivations. For example, one part of you might be trying to lose weight, and another part might want to eat whatever it wants. We can all recognize parts like the Inner Critic, the Abandoned Child, the Pleaser, the Angry Part, and the Loving Caretaker.

Parts have motivations for everything they do. Nothing is done just out of habit. Nothing is just a pattern of thinking or behavior that you learned. Everything (except for purely physiological reactions) is done by a part for a reason, even though that reason may be unconscious.

Understanding parts in this way gives you a great deal of power to change your inner system. It means that there is an understandable rationale for your behavior, feelings, and attitudes. It is possible to get to know these parts, develop relationships with them, and help them heal. Once healed, they no longer need to behave in ways that seem at odds with your intentions, values, and goals. The possibility for harmonious integration is real.

Richard Schwartz, PhD, in developing the IFS method, discovered that every part has a positive intent for you, no matter how problematic its behavior. For example, Bill had a part that was judgmental and competitive with other people in a way that was not consistent with his true values. However, when he really got to know that part, he discovered that it was just trying to help him feel OK about himself in the only way it knew how—by feeling superior to others.

Understanding that a part has positive intent doesn't mean that you give the part power. Bill doesn't want his part to act out being judgmental and competitive. Using the IFS approach, Bill can relate to this part with understanding and appreciation while also taking the steps to heal it.

This approach is fundamentally different from the way we ordinarily relate to our parts. Usually when we become aware of a part, the first thing we do is evaluate it. Is it good or bad for us? If we decide it is good, we embrace it and give it power. If we decide it is bad, we try to suppress it or get rid of it. The truth is, you can't get rid of a part. You can only push it into the deeper layers of your psyche, where it will continue to affect you without your awareness.

In IFS, we do something altogether different and radical. We welcome all our parts with curiosity and compassion. We seek to understand them and appreciate their efforts to help us. We develop a relationship of caring and trust with each part and then take the steps to release it from its burdens so it can function in a healthy way.

In the IFS system, Protectors are the parts you usually encounter first in exploring yourself. Their job is to handle the world, protect you, and keep you functioning. They interact in a reasonable, strategic way with the people, responsibilities, and situations in your environment. The other main function of these parts is to protect you from the pain of the Exiles. These are young child parts that hold the pain from the past. They are generally exiled, or kept out of consciousness, by the Protectors.

In the above example, Bill had a Protector that was competitive and judgmental toward others. It was trying to help Bill feel superior in order to protect against an Exile Part that felt inadequate. The Exile Part had probably suffered some kind of humiliation or rejection in the past that left it feeling unworthy.

Parts take on these dysfunctional roles because of what has happened to them in the past. Exiles take on pain and burdens from what they experienced as children. Protectors take on their roles in order to protect Exiles or to protect you from the pain of Exiles.

The IFS Process

IFS has a method of understanding and working with these parts to release the burdens they carry from the past and heal the system so you can function in healthy ways. The key to this healing is the Self. IFS recognizes that each of us has a spiritual center—a true Self. This Self is naturally compassionate and curious about people, especially about our own parts. The Self wants to connect with each part and get to know and understand it. The Self feels compassion for the pain of the Exiles and the burdens of pain that they carry. It also has compassion for the Protectors and the tough jobs they take on trying to keep the Exiles from being reinjured or exposed. The Self is able to stay calm and centered despite the sometimes intense emotions that parts may feel. Everyone has a Self, even though you may feel that yours is not very accessible at times because of the activity of your parts.

The Self is the agent of healing—the true leader of the internal system that can love and heal each part. The first step in the IFS process is learning how to access the Self. Then the Self focuses its energy on the part. In Bill's case, he started out his IFS work by focusing on his Judgmental Part. With some work, he was able to be genuinely in his Self so that he was interested in getting to know the Judgmental Part. He found out that it was trying to protect an Exile Part of him that felt inadequate. Bill had a learning problem as a child, even though he is quite intelligent and competent. So there was a young part of Bill that had felt inadequate in school. The Judgmental Part was trying to compensate for this inadequate experience by feeling superior to people. Bill had grown up in a judgmental, competitive home, so that was the primary model this part knew. As Bill got to know the Judgmental Part, he understood why this part acted as it did and appreciated its efforts on his behalf.

He then contacted the Exile who felt inadequate. He listened and watched as this part showed him scenes from his childhood when it felt ashamed and inadequate because of his learning problem, and he responded to the Exile with compassion and caring. The young part responded to this by feeling cherished and valuable for the first time. Up until then, it had been hidden away in Bill's unconscious, which only increased its feelings of worthlessness. With love from Bill's Self, this young part was able to release the burden of inadequacy that it had been carrying and feel good about itself. This allowed the Judgmental Protector to relax. It no longer needed to judge people to compensate for the Exile's pain. This enabled Bill to respond to people in the way he always wanted—with openness, acceptance, and a cooperative attitude.

IFS Principles

The following are some basic principles of the Internal Family Systems Model. These concepts underlie the work described in this workbook.

- All parts are welcome.

- You never **make** a part step aside or separate—you only ask.

- You respect the reasons parts have for what they are and aren't willing to do.

- All parts have positive intent at their core and ultimately want only the best for you. If they appear to have negative intent, they are using strategies that, on some level, made sense at some point in their past but are no longer effective. Getting inside their world and understanding the origin of those strategies is a key step in helping them adopt more effective strategies.

- Parts will cooperate once their fears are addressed and once they can feel you in Self and understand your intentions.

- It isn't possible to do it wrong when working on yourself using IFS. Even if your process is completely blocked, it just means that a Protector is stopping the process for some reason. You access that Protector and find out why it is behaving that way.

- The fastest way to resolve an issue is to work slowly, patiently, and respectfully with all parts involved.

Chapter 2

GUIDED MEDITATIONS

A guided meditation is an audio journey that evokes an altered state of consciousness during which material from the deeper layers of your psyche is more readily available to you. Three audio recordings of guided meditations are included with this book:

- Getting into Self
- Appreciating Protectors
- Soothing a Triggered Exile

They can be accessed at http://personal-growth-programs.com/self-therapy-workbook-bonnie-weiss/. The transcripts for these meditations are located in Appendix B.

When doing this kind of imagery exercise, it is best to sit or lie in a completely relaxed, comfortable position. Never listen to guided imagery while driving or doing anything that requires full alert attention. If you discover that you have a tendency to fall asleep during guided meditations, it is best to maintain an upright sitting position without head support. This will keep you awake while still allowing deep relaxation. It is especially important to use this position after eating a big meal or if you are tired.

The best attitude to adopt for guided meditations is a combination of letting go and staying focused. Letting go allows images from the deeper layers of your psyche to emerge freely. There is no need to try to control the images or sensations that you feel or the words that you hear. It's important not to doubt or discard whatever spontaneously emerges. You might be inclined to discard something because you don't understand it or you think it is unacceptable. Sometimes it is actually a plus to have something emerge that is not immediately clear. Some of the most important information from our psyche isn't readily understandable. When we allow ourselves to be with things we're initially inclined to reject, new avenues of self-understanding can emerge. Please trust that the image or other information has come up for a good reason and that you don't need to fear your psyche.

The other important ability is staying focused. This means keeping on track with the meditation directions as well as with the thread of your own inner journey. During meditation, it is easy to "space out" or daydream about irrelevant issues. This happens to almost everyone from time to time. If you find that you have lost focus, don't become worried or judge yourself—just gently bring yourself back to the track of the meditation.

Don't assume that all imagery has to be visual. Some people don't visualize very well but are good at body imagery. They can sense body feelings, posture, and movement, and they may also imagine their body in different shapes. This is called kinesthetic imagery. Some people have profound meditative experiences this way. Other people mainly get information through hearing voices, words, or sounds. So if you have trouble visualizing, just notice what information is coming through these other channels.

Chapter 3

THE SELF

*A downloadable guided meditation that facilitates
getting into Self is available in MP3 format at
http://personal-growth-programs.com/self-therapy-workbook-bonnie-weiss/*

Fortunately, human beings are not simply a collection of parts. We are so much more than that. Our true Self is mature and loving, and has the capacity to heal and integrate our parts.

We each have a core aspect of us that is our true self and our spiritual center. When our extreme parts are not activated and getting in the way, we have access to this core, which is who we really are. The Self is relaxed, open, and accepting of others and ourselves. When we are in Self, we are grounded, centered, and nonreactive. We don't get triggered by what people do. We remain calm and unruffled, even in difficult circumstances. The Self is so much larger and more spacious than our parts and is not frightened by events that would scare parts. When we are in Self, we are the shining center of the system that is each of us.

The IFS Model talks about the eight C's that are the principal qualities of the Self. They are: Compassion, Curiosity, Connection, Calm, Courage, Clarity, Caring, and Creativity. The four capacities described on the next page are the most relevant for doing an IFS session.

Self Capacities

♥ Compassion   ♥ Courage

♥ Curiosity   **Self**   ♥ Clarity

♥ Connection   ♥ Caring

♥ Calm   ♥ Creativity

1. **The Self is connected.** When you are in Self, you naturally feel close to other people and want to relate in harmonious, supportive ways. You are drawn to make contact with them and to be in community. The Self also wants to be connected to your parts. When you are in Self, you are interested in having a relationship with each of your parts, which helps them trust you and opens the way for healing.

2. **The Self is curious.** When you are in Self, you are curious about other people in an open, accepting way. When you inquire into what makes them tick, it's because you want to understand them, not judge them. The Self is also curious about the inner workings of your mind. You want to understand why each part acts as it does, what its positive intent is for you, and what it is trying to protect you from. This curiosity comes from an accepting place, not a critical one. When parts sense this genuine interest, they know they are entering a welcoming environment, and they aren't afraid to reveal themselves to you.

3. **The Self is compassionate.** Compassion is a form of kindness and love that arises when people are in pain. You genuinely care about how others feel and often feel prompted to support them through difficult times. When you are in Self, you also naturally feel compassion for yourself. When parts are extreme, they're reacting to pain; Exiles feel it, and Protectors try to avoid it. Compassion toward yourself is the most essential ingredient in the inner quest for understanding. It is needed in order to hold, support, and nurture your parts while you explore your system. Your parts can sense the Self's compassion. It makes them feel safe and cared for, so they want to open up and share themselves with you.

4. **The Self is calm, centered, and grounded.** This is especially helpful when you are relating to a part that has intense emotions. Intense grief or shame, for example, can be overwhelming if you aren't grounded in Self. Protectors will avoid a part that has very strong emotions. But when you are centered in the calmness of Self, there is no need to avoid a part that is feeling intense emotion. You remain in Self while the part shows you its pain. The calmness of Self supports you through the difficult work of witnessing and healing the part.

For all these reasons, the Self is the agent of psychological healing in IFS work. It helps you heal and transform your parts so they become free of their extreme feelings and behavior, and can assume healthy roles in your life.

The Structure of the Psyche

The Self is also the natural leader of your internal system and the natural occupant of the "seat of consciousness." It has the courage to take risks, the perspective to see reality clearly, and the creativity to find good solutions to problems. The Self is balanced and fair, and it sees what needs to happen in most situations. When you have healed your parts and they trust you, they finally allow the Self to lead. Ideally the Self is the one who makes decisions and moves the system forward. The Self is the conductor of the orchestra, the one who brings in the woodwinds at the right time, tells the musicians when to play softly, and cues the horn solo. It chooses the best course of action in each moment and calls on your healthy parts to contribute their gifts. Your parts trust the Self and rely on its wisdom.

The goal of IFS work is to unburden each part so it has a healthy role and for each part to trust the Self to lead. Because the Self is the leader of the internal system, it can be trusted to move the system toward wholeness. The Self can work with each part to release its burdens and transform.

Self Meditation

The following guided meditation can be used to access your Self. You can read this meditation, periodically stopping to sit with your eyes closed and allowing the words to evoke sensations and images. You can also record it with your own voice or have a friend read it to you. An additional Getting into Self Meditation that is part of this workbook can be found at http://personal-growth-programs.com/self-therapy-workbook-bonnie-weiss/ and is transcribed in Appendix B.

A guided meditation is a journey that evokes an altered state of consciousness. When doing this kind of imagery exercise, it is best to sit or lie in a completely relaxed, comfortable position. Always give it your full, undivided attention. Allow yourself time to experience the images on both the physical and emotional levels. Trust whatever comes up for you as being exactly what you need in this moment. There is no right or wrong—just experience and information. Enjoy.

Introductory Meditation Text

Close your eyes. Go inside …

and begin by focusing on your body sensations …

just noticing wherever your attention goes in your body …

in each moment … and being with that sensation.

Whether it's a tingling in your hands …

or a quivering in your closed eyelids …

or a relaxation in your belly …

or tension in your shoulders …

whatever it is, be present with that sensation.

And then, as time goes on, your attention may move

to a different part of your body …

and just allow yourself to be present with that sensation.

And as you do that, allow it to relax you … and take you deeper inside.

Just continuing to be with your body … deepening into yourself.

And now focus your attention on your belly … the sensations in your belly.

Whether it's a fullness … or a softness … or a solidness …

or just the sense of the rise and fall of your belly with each breath …

or something altogether different.

Whatever it is, just be present with the sensations in your belly …

and allow them to take you into that center place in your consciousness …

anchoring you … in your belly … coming to a grounded, solid place inside yourself.

Okay … now gradually, begin to bring yourself back from this deep place

that you've been …

beginning to deepen your breathing …

wiggle around a little bit … open your eyes …

and come back to your regular waking consciousness.

WORKING WITH PROTECTORS

P1. Accessing a Part

P2. Unblending from a Target Part

P3. Checking for Self-Leadership
& Unblending from a Concerned Part

P4. Getting to Know a Protector

P5. Developing a Trusting
Relationship with a Protector

Chapter 4

ACCESSING PARTS

*A downloadable guided meditation that covers
the material in Chapters 4–8 is available in MP3 format at
http://personal-growth-programs.com/self-therapy-workbook-bonnie-weiss/*

Trailhead

Let's suppose you have an issue you would like to work on. How do you know what parts to explore? In IFS, issues are sometimes referred to as trailheads. A *trailhead* is an experience or a difficulty in your life that will lead to interesting parts if you follow it. It can be a situation or person that you react to, an emotional or bodily experience, a pattern of behavior or thinking, a dream, or anything else that indicates one or more parts to explore. IFS calls it a trailhead because it is the beginning of a trail that can lead to healing. It usually involves both a life situation and your response to that situation.

Accessing a Part

You begin an IFS session by accessing a part that you believe will be helpful to work with. It might be related to an important trailhead, or it might be causing you intense feelings in the moment. The emphasis in this chapter is on how to make simple contact with the part. Getting to know the part fully will be covered in succeeding chapters. We are starting with Protectors.

It is best to close your eyes during this process and for the rest of any IFS session. We also recommend doing this work in a private room where you won't be disturbed by people, pets, phones, or computers. This cuts down on distractions and allows you to focus completely on the Protector you are accessing.

Part Activation

A part is **activated** when its extreme feelings or beliefs are triggered by a situation or person. You can feel that the part is here, present with you.

Target Part

This is the part you are focusing on or working with.

Ways to Access a Part

Emotion: How it feels emotionally

Visual: An image of the part

Body: Sensing the part in your body

Verbal: Listening for what the part says to you

Name for part: A descriptive phrase, person's name, character, animal, and so on

The body sense is often the most direct route for accessing a part, but it is not completely necessary for making contact and getting information. A part can show up as a sensation in or around your body. It can be a chronic sensation, like a stiff neck, or a habitual way of holding your arm, or it can be a sensation that arises in the moment as you pay attention to the part, like an emptiness in your chest, a queasy feeling in your belly, or a sudden headache.

When you access a part, try for as many channels of information as you can because they each have value, but you only *need* one of the above.

Once you have accessed a part through one or more channels, allow a word or phrase to arise that describes the part as you are experiencing it. You might ask the part how it would describe itself.

Three Ways to Begin a Session

1 Having a specific part in mind
2. Working with a trailhead
3 Starting with your current experience

1. Working with a specific part

Think of a part that you are interested in getting to know. Check to see if the part is activated at the moment. You can tell if the part is present in the moment by noticing if you can see or feel it. Do you easily see the world from its point of view and feel its emotions?

When a part isn't activated

If that part isn't activated, think of a recent situation when the part was activated. Imagine yourself in that situation right now.

EXERCISE   **Accessing a Part That Isn't Activated**

Choose one of your parts that isn't activated right now. Take a moment, close your eyes, deepen your breath, and imagine that you are in a situation in which the part is activated. Notice how it feels to be there. From that place, try accessing the part using each of the channels—feeling, image, body, and internal voice. Write down what you experience.

Name of part: _perfectionism_

The situation that activates the part: _Chaos, + feeling like I'm not working hard enough_

What the part feels emotionally: _tight chest - sadness, tightness_

What it looks like: _scream? tight face_

What it feels like in your body: _tight chest_

What the part says: _I feel safe when everything is in order + there is no mess / chaos_

﹡ Remember that it isn't necessary to achieve access through all channels.

SAMPLE   **Accessing a Part That Isn't Activated**

Name of part: <u>Perfectionist</u>

The situation that activates the part: <u>Finding a rip in my backpack</u>

What the part feels emotionally: <u>I feel safer when things are perfect.</u>

What it looks like: <u>A perfect box, all sides completely the same, with</u>
<u>right angles all equal in size</u>

What it feels like in your body: <u>Tension in my chest</u>

What the part says: <u>I like to be safe, and I feel safe when everything is</u>
<u>the way that it should be. I feel safe when there is a sense of harmony,</u>
<u>wholeness, and evenness, and everything is the same.</u>

---

2. Identifying the Parts at a Trailhead

Think of an issue or situation that you are interested in exploring.

Imagine yourself in that situation or with that person or having that experience.

Notice a part that is activated and access it.

Now ask that part to step aside so you can see what other parts are there.

Notice another part that is activated and access it.

Repeat until no new parts are activated by that trailhead.

Trailhead Questions:

Here are a few questions you can ask at a trailhead to identify the parts:

- What is the main feeling or part in this situation?
- Is there another part that feels differently or opposes that part?
- Are there any feelings of self-judgment or critics that are reacting to the situation?
- Is there any other part that would like its voice to be heard on this issue?

EXERCISE **Identifying the Parts at a Trailhead**

Choose a trailhead that you are interested in exploring. If it is not current in your life, take a moment to close your eyes and imagine you are in that situation now. Ask yourself, "What parts are here as I connect with this situation or look at this issue?" List the parts at this trailhead one by one as they arise. For each part, write as much of the following information as you can. Remember, you haven't fully explored these parts, so don't be concerned if you don't know much about them. Just fill in what you know. You can add more information later.

Name of part: _____

What the part feels emotionally: _____

What it looks like: _____

What it feels like in your body and where: _____

What the part says: _____

How it makes you behave: _____

What it wants: _____

SAMPLE **Identifying the Parts at a Trailhead**

Situation: <u>Someone elbowed me on a bus.</u>

Name of Part 1: <u>Anger</u>

What the part feels emotionally: <u>Disrespected, fiery</u>

What it looks like: <u>Smoky-nosed dragon</u>

What it feels like in your body and where: <u>Face, tight jaw, burning eyes</u>

What the part says: <u>I hate you.</u>

How it makes you behave: <u>Mean and grouchy</u>

What it wants: <u>To protect itself</u>

Sample continued on next page

Sample continued from previous page

Name of Part 2: Judgment

What the part feels emotionally: Self-righteous

What it looks like: Snarky old man pointing a finger

What it feels like in your body and where: Tension in midsection, raised shoulder

What the part says: You idiot. How could you be so thoughtless? You are so selfish. Pay attention to what you are doing.

How it makes you behave: Shaking my head, scoffing, name-calling

What it wants: The other person to feel small and stupid, and go away

Name of Part 3: Fear

What the part feels emotionally: I am not safe here.

What it looks like: Someone cowering

What it feels like in your body and where: Shivering all over

What the part says: I am not safe here. It is unpredictable. Anything could happen. I could get hurt.

How it makes you behave: Shrinking away, looking around warily

What it wants: Safety, protection, help

Name of Part 4: Physically hurt

What the part feels emotionally: Sad, pained

What it looks like: Child crying

What it feels like in your body and where: Contracted where struck, face contorted

What the part says: Oww, that hurts.

How it makes you behave: Crying and letting it out

What it wants: Someone to comfort it

3. *Starting with your current experience*

The third way to access a part is by staying present in the moment and exploring what parts are there. Turn your attention to your current experience and see what parts you notice. What emotions are you feeling, what internal messages do you hear, and what body sensations or tensions come into your awareness? Assume that all of these are from parts. Feel into an emotion or body sensation and see what gradually emerges.

EXERCISE   Identifying the Parts in Your Current Experience

Take a moment to close your eyes, deepen your breath, and focus inward. Ask yourself, "What parts are here in my current awareness? What emotions am I feeling? What thoughts or messages am I telling myself? What body sensations are present?" One by one as they arise, write them down. For each part, write as much of the following information as you can. As before, you haven't fully explored these parts, so don't worry if you only know a little about them.

Name of part: _____

What it feels emotionally: _____

_____

What it looks like: _____

What it feels like in your body and where: _____

_____

What the part says: _____

How it makes you behave: _____

What it wants: _____

_____

SAMPLE   **Identifying the Parts in Your Current Experience**

Name of Part 1: Anxiety

What it feels emotionally: Worried about upcoming meeting

What it looks like: TV static

What it feels like in your body and where: Jazziness in chest and belly

What the part says: You're not prepared. They're not going to like you.

How it makes you behave: Hyperactive, distracted

What it wants: To run away

Name of Part 2: Critic

What it feels emotionally: Angry at me

What it looks like: Harsh mother

What it feels like in your body and where: Tight jaw, tension in arms, contracted chest, pointing finger

What the part says: You didn't prepare. You wasted time. You're lazy!

How it makes you behave: Agitated, disorganized

What it wants: For me to focus and get something done

Name of Part 3: Scared child

What it feels emotionally: Afraid of being found to be inadequate and then rejected

What it looks like: Five-year-old cowering in the corner

What it feels like in your body and where: Hands over head, crying

What the part says: I'm sorry I'm not good enough.

How it makes you behave: Scared and withdrawn

What it wants: To feel safe and accepted

EXERCISE   Noticing a Part in Real Time

This is an exercise you can do during the week as homework practice.

Choose a part that gets activated with some frequency in your life that you want to learn more about. You might take a moment and let that part know in some way that you're interested in getting to know it better.

Name of part: _____

What it feels emotionally: _____

_____

What it looks like: _____

What it feels like in your body and where: _____

_____

What the part says: _____

How it makes you behave: _____

What it wants: _____

_____

Noticing the Part

Over the next week, practice noticing when this part is activated. It will help to know what cues will tip you off that it is activated. What body sensations, thoughts, or emotions will let you know it is up—for example, a tight stomach, revenge fantasies, or feeling teary like a child? _____

_____

_____

_____

What behavior will cue you that this part has taken over—for example, withdrawing from your partner, taking over a conversation, or eating too much? _____

_____

What situations or people tend to activate this part—for example, meeting someone you are attracted to, giving a talk, or being disobeyed by your son? _____

_____

When are these likely to occur during the next week? _____

_____

Set an intention to be especially aware of whether this part becomes activated during those times. Each time you notice that the part is triggered, access it briefly and take a few notes about it. If you can't stop in the moment to take notes, do it at your next break or as soon as you can so it will be fresh in your memory. At the end of each day, take a few minutes to review the day for moments when the part was activated. Add to your notes at this time. This daily review will also help you keep this exercise in mind the following day.

Notes to take each time it happens:

Situation: _____

How you experience the part: _____

What about this situation triggered the part: _____

_____

Don't expect perfection. You probably won't catch all the times this part is activated or be clear about what is going on each time. That is very difficult to do. You may be driving or trying to get a project finished or talking with someone, for example, so it may be difficult to be aware of much else. That's fine—just do the best you can.

SAMPLE   **Noticing a Part in Real Time**

Part: <u>Indulger</u>

What it feels emotionally: <u>Wild and out of control</u>

What it looks like: <u>A big mouth</u>

What it feels like in your body and where: <u>Like an empty hole in my belly</u>
<u>that needs filling</u>

What the part says: <u>I won't stop. I need more and more.</u>

How it makes you behave: <u>It eats out of control. It eats foods that are not</u>
<u>healthy for me and doesn't stop when I am full.</u>

What it wants: <u>To keep filling up an empty hole so I don't feel any</u>
<u>emotional pain</u>

Noticing the Part

What behavior will cue you that the part has taken over? <u>Finishing a meal</u>
<u>and taking seconds, even though I am not hungry anymore. Snacking</u>
<u>between meals right out of the refrigerator. Buying junk food when</u>
<u>I know I shouldn't eat it.</u>

What situations or people tend to activate this part? <u>Family members, holidays,</u>
<u>stressful situations where I am afraid I will be judged. Being alone.</u>

When are these likely to occur during the next week? <u>Pressure at work.</u>
<u>Having no plans for the weekend.</u>

Chapter 5

UNBLENDING & CONSCIOUS BLENDING

Unblending from the Target Part

A part is blended with Self when you are flooded with the feelings of the part in such a way that you aren't grounded. You are caught up in the beliefs of the part and see things from its point of view. You are not separate enough from the part to be able to witness it or be with it. To access a part in a useful way, you want it to be activated but not blended.

The Self is the natural occupant of the "seat of consciousness" (see page 11). When you are blended, the part rather than the Self resides in the seat (below left). In order to make productive contact with the part, you want the Self to be in the seat and the part to be the focus of its attention (below right).

As mentioned earlier, the part you are currently focusing your attention on is the Target Part.

A part in the
seat of consciousness

Self in the
seat of consciousness

EXERCISE   Blending

Choose a part of you that you are blended with in this moment. Take a moment to close your eyes and see what is here. Ask yourself, "What am I aware of thinking or feeling in this moment?" How strongly are you feeling the part's feelings right now?

It will probably be a part that you identify with as part of your personality. It could be a part that motivates you to do things in your normal day, a part that criticizes you or judges others, or a part that gets angry or reactive when things happen, such as spilling your coffee or losing your keys. It could be a part that organizes you, or worries you, or needs something from someone else, or any other regular part that shows up in your life.

What does it feel like in your body when that part is here?

What is tense? _____

What is relaxed? _____

What sensations are you aware of? _____

Is your visual focus open or closed? _____

What parts of your body are you unaware of? For example, are you only in your head? Only feeling your belly? _____

What is your breath like? _____

What emotions are here? (For example, anger, frustration, impatience, lovingkindness, generosity, urgency, others) _____

What are your thoughts? _____

What are you saying to yourself? _____

What is held as true from this part's point of view? (For example: I have a lot of responsibilities to fulfill and I have to keep working to fulfill them, or I never get what I need from this person, or There's never enough time.) _____

_____

SAMPLE   **Blending**

What is tense? <u>Jaw, upper chest</u>

What is relaxed? <u>Legs</u>

What sensations are you aware of? <u>Shortness of breath, shoulder up</u>

Is your visual focus open or closed? <u>Narrow, intense</u>

What parts of your body are you unaware of? <u>Midback, genitals</u>

What is your breath like? <u>Constricted</u>

What emotions are here? <u>Anger, frustration</u>

What are your thoughts? <u>Feeling resentful and obsessing about a hurtful act against me</u>

What are you saying to yourself? <u>I don't deserve this. Who do they think they are?</u>

What is held as true from this part's point of view? <u>I have been wronged!</u>

Unblending

Unblending happens when you create space between you and a Target Part. You are asking the Target Part to cooperate with you to make some emotional space so you can be more present with it. You want the part to understand that you are interested in getting to know it and that the most effective way to do that is if you have a little distance from it.

You can decide to unblend when you become aware that a part is seated in the "seat of consciousness" rather than the Self. You are attempting to bring the Self into the seat of consciousness and have the Target Part be the focus of its attention (see right-hand illustration on page 27).

EXERCISE   **Unblending from a Target Part**

You may use the part that you explored in the previous exercise (page 28), or you may want to get to know a different part. If so, go through the steps previously outlined until the part you are interested in is present. Let the part know in some way that you are interested in getting to know it.

Name or role of part: _____

How you know you are blended: _____

Here is a list of questions or actions that can help the unblending process.

- Ask the part to separate from you so you can get to know it.
- Ask the part to move out of your body.
- Ask the part to contain its feelings and not flood you while you focus on it.
- Move back to separate from the part.
- Notice how you feel toward the part.
- Get an image of the part at a distance from you.
- Do a short centering/grounding meditation to support your separateness from the part.

How you asked your Target Part to separate: _____

When a part separates, you will notice a shift. This can be any of a number of possible subtle changes in your awareness of it.

- You may feel an opening in your body and a sense of space and openness.
- You may see it move, for example, the image of the part moves farther away from you.
- You might hear it agree to your request.
- You might feel emotionally lighter or freer.

What you noticed when you asked your Target Part to give you a little space:

_____

_____

What you noticed if your part agreed to unblend:

What the part said: _____

Bodily changes: _____

Visual shifts: _____

Emotional changes: _____

Anything else: _____

_____

S A M P L E   **Unblending from a Target Part**

Name or role of part: <u>Procrastinator</u>

How you know you are blended: <u>Feeling antsy and distracted, avoiding</u>
   <u>work that has to be done by cleaning kitchen or surfing the Internet</u>

How you asked your Target Part to separate: <u>I told it that I recognized it</u>
   <u>was here to make me avoid my work. I asked if it would work with me</u>
   <u>so that I could accomplish something, and then we could play.</u>

What you noticed when you asked your Target Part to give you a little space:
   <u>At first it was resistant, pretending it didn't exist with a "what—who,</u>
   <u>me?" attitude. Then it became interested in my promise to spend time</u>
   <u>with it later.</u>

What you noticed if your part agreed to unblend:

What the part said: <u>"You'd better keep your promise to give me time later."</u>

Bodily changes: <u>I was able to settle down a little. I felt calmer, and my</u>
   <u>breathing deepened.</u>

Visual shifts: <u>I was better able to focus.</u>

Emotional changes: <u>I felt the fear underneath the distraction.</u>

Anything else: <u>Once I felt and recognized the fear, it subsided a little.</u>

EXERCISE **Reluctance to Unblend** (extension of previous exercise)

Sometimes parts are reluctant to separate. They may be confused about what it means to unblend, or they may be frightened or stubborn. A good question to ask a hesitant part is, "What are you afraid would happen if you did separate?" It can be useful to reassure the part that you're not trying to get rid of it or make it go away—that you want to be able to listen to it better, and a little separation will allow you to do that.

Here are some typical reasons that parts are reluctant to separate. If the part that you have been working with in the previous exercises is hesitant to unblend, you can check off any reasons that apply or add your own.

_____ Fear that you will push it aside and not need it anymore.

Possible answer: I'm asking you to step aside for a short time while I explore this issue. I want to get to know you, and I need some separation from you to do that. You can come back in your old way, if you like, when we are done.

In addition: You may need to validate that you *have* pushed the part away in the past and that this time *is* different.

_____ Fear that you will do something unwise that it is protecting you from doing.

Possible answer: Reassure it that you are only asking for a defined period of time. Remind it that you are here and that you will make sure that nothing bad happens.

Other fears: _____

_____

Your responses to your part: _____

_____

What you said to your part to help it feel more comfortable with unblending:

_____

_____

How the part responded:

What the part said: _____

Bodily changes: _____

Visual shifts: _____

Emotional changes: _____

Anything else: _____

EXERCISE Daily Parts Check-In

For the next week, take a little time each day to check in with your parts. Notice which parts are activated at that moment, as you learned to do in this section. By doing this regularly, you will get used to paying attention to your inner family. Plan a certain time each day to do this exercise. Some people prefer to do it first thing in the morning, others at night before they go to bed. Make a list of each part that is activated at that time. For each one, fill in the following answers, if you know them:

Name of part: _____

What it feels: _____

What it looks like: _____

Where it is located in your body: _____

What the part says: _____

_____

How it makes you behave: _____

_____

✳ Don't be concerned if you don't know all this information about the part. Just fill in what you can.

SAMPLE **Daily Parts Check-In**

Monday morning

Name of part: Anxiety

What it feels: Fear that I won't be able to face the day

What it looks like: Shaking, quivering little boy

Where it is located in your body: Pounding in my chest, stomach tension, hiding my head

What it says: I won't be able to do this or that. I won't have the energy. I won't be able to figure it out. Life is overwhelming.

How it makes you behave: Not move, frozen, just stay under the covers

Thursday night

Name of part: Relieved

What it feels: Grateful I got through the day. Relaxed and at peace. Thankful it's over.

What it looks like: Peaceful child sleeping

Where it is located in your body: Lack of tension all over

What it says: I did it. I got through it. I got through the day.

How it makes you behave: Can relax and recover

Conscious Blending

We've discussed how blending interferes with being in Self and discussed ways to unblend from a part. However, there are times when it can be useful to consciously blend with a part. This is done purposely and with the permission of the Self. It is only safe when you are solidly in Self. Here are three ways:

1. Accessing a part by speaking as it

If you are having trouble accessing a part or you want to get a fuller experience of the part, you can consciously blend with the part by speaking as the part—just the opposite of what was suggested before. This allows you to become the part for a while and feel it more fully. You can negotiate with a part to modulate or tone down its feelings when you blend with it.

2. Accessing a part using body expression

You can also access a part more fully by becoming the part and expressing it through body movement, expression, and sound. This allows you to more fully embody the part and therefore understand it more completely.

3. Feeling a part's emotions

As discussed under Unblending from an Exile (Chapter 12), it can foster fuller witnessing of a part to allow yourself to feel its emotions as long as this doesn't take you out of Self. This can lead to a deeper level of healing.

EXERCISE   Conscious Blending

This exercise is best done with a partner or small group. Each person works for ten minutes. After everyone has had a turn, spend some time giving each other feedback about your experience while each person was exploring a part. Make sure your feedback is about your own experience. It is helpful to use parts language when giving feedback. This means speaking for the parts of you that came up as you saw each person work.

Choose a part to work with that you feel comfortable blending with.

1. Speak as the part: "I am . . . and I feel . . ."
2. Act out the part's feelings or its nature without words. Do so through body movement, facial expression, and sound.
3. Check with the part to see if you represented it well.
4. Speak for it: "The part feels . . ."

Use the space below to make notes on your experience.

Part: _____

What it had to say: _____

Nonverbal ways it expressed itself: _____

How it felt I represented it: _____

Chapter 6

CHECKING FOR SELF-LEADERSHIP & UNBLENDING FROM CONCERNED PARTS

What Is Self-Leadership?

As described earlier, being in Self means that you are experiencing one or more of the Self qualities as your present state. If you feel compassionate, curious, or caring, you are experiencing Self-leadership, or are "in Self," as IFS calls it. In other words, the real you is sitting in the "seat of consciousness." From this place, it is safe to proceed to get to know the Target Part.

Why Check for Self-Leadership?

Usually when we are aware of parts of ourselves, we evaluate them. We embrace the parts that we like and approve of, and we often identify with parts that we see as positive. We reject the parts that we see as problematic. IFS encourages us to do neither but instead to be open and interested in getting to know each part of ourselves. To do this effectively, we want to be in Self.

Concerned Part

A Concerned Part is a part that is blended with Self that has concerns about the Target Part. It interferes with your ability to be in Self with respect to the Target Part (see illustration on next page).

Concerned Parts have agendas and opinions. If, for example, you feel angry or judgmental toward the Target Part, or scared of it, or if you want to get rid of it, that attitude is coming from another part. It is important to identify these parts in order to make open contact with the Target Part from Self.

❶ Concerned Part in the
seat of consciousness

How Do You Check for Concerned Parts?

In IFS, you ask the magic question "How do I feel toward the Target Part now?"

Then you allow space inside and see what comes up. The question is not meant to elicit an evaluation of the part or your opinion about it. The purpose is to find out how you feel emotionally toward the part. You're not asking how you feel toward the part in general or at other times when it is activated—only how you feel toward it right now as you are making contact with it.

❷ Self in the seat
of consciousness,
focusing on the
Concerned Part

Unblending from a Concerned Part

Before you can work effectively on the Target Part, you need to unblend from the Concerned Parts so that you can be in Self with the Target Part.

❸ Self in the seat of consciousness, focusing on the Target Part

Being in Self with the Target Part

You are in Self when you feel open, curious, compassionate, or appreciative toward the Target Part. Examples of these experiences might be:

- **Open:** I feel nothing special. There is a spaciousness where my Concerned Part used to be. I am neutral and ready to engage.

- **Curious:** I feel separate from the part and genuinely interested in who it is and what it has to tell or teach me.

- **Compassionate:** I can see more clearly who this part is, what it has been holding, and why it has behaved the way it has.

- **Appreciative:** I see how hard this part has been working for me. I understand in this moment why it is here and the job it has been doing.

EXERCISE   Unblending from a Concerned Part

For this exercise, choose a Protector that you don't like or have some strong feelings about. For example, you might have a part that gets angry easily and interferes with your relationships with friends, or you might have a part that eats too much even though you're trying to be healthy or watch your weight. You would naturally have reactions to parts like these. You might judge them or be angry at them and want to get rid of them. You might also feel distant from them or scared of them. Any of these attitudes that arise are coming from a Concerned Part of you.

Take a moment to choose a Protector Part that you are interested in knowing more about. First, access the Protector (Step P1, page 15) and then unblend as much as you can from it (Step P2, page 27). This Protector will be your Target Part.

Take note of what is going on in your body and how the part is responding to you as you come in contact with it. _____

_____

Ask the magic question, "How do I feel toward the Target Part now?"

What do you notice—anger, frustration, wanting the part to go away? Any of these responses is a Concerned Part. Fill in the chart with your answers.

Concerned Part	Concerned Part	Concerned Part
Name: _____	Name: _____	Name: _____

Target Part

Name: _____

If you happen to feel open, curious, or compassionate about the part, you are probably in Self. Since the exercise asked you to choose a part that you have difficulty with, coming from Self at this point in the exercise is unlikely.

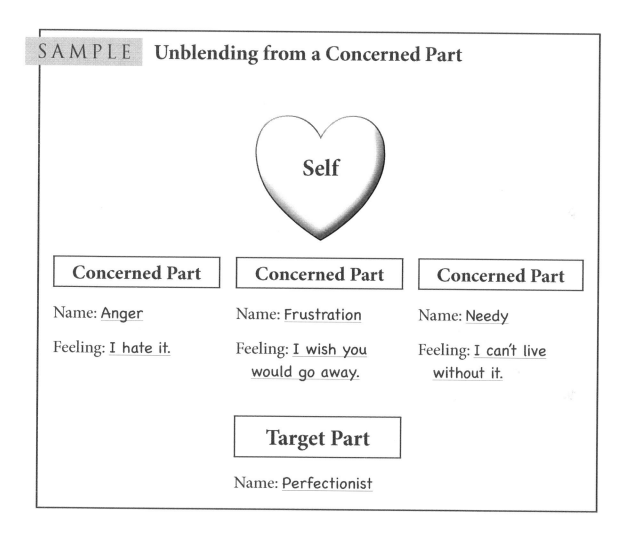

Asking Concerned Parts to Relax

Ask the Concerned Part if it would be willing to step aside (or relax) just for now so you can get to know the Target Part from an open place. The Concerned Part may agree or disagree.

1. Concerned Part Willing to Relax: If it agrees, you may feel a shift in your body such as a relaxing or an opening. You may see an image of the part moving away. You may hear the part's voice saying that it will relax, or it may do some negotiating about its willingness to step aside or relax.

As each part in your original list relaxes, ask again, "How do I feel toward the Target Part?"

Sometimes it's helpful to say something like, "Now that the anger and frustration have stepped aside, how do I feel toward the part?" If you find another Concerned Part, repeat the process until you are in Self and you feel a sense of open space, curiosity, or compassion.

From here, you can begin to get to know the Target Part from a place of Self.

2. Concerned Part Unwilling to Relax: If a Concerned Part isn't willing to step aside, you can explain to it the value of stepping aside. You might say something like:

"I sincerely want to help this part (Target Part). I see that it needs healing. I want to get to know it. I recognize that the only way to do that effectively is from an open, curious place. I would appreciate it if you would allow me the space to make contact with it from this place of Self."

Listen carefully to the Concerned Part's fears and reassure it. See page 32 for parts' typical fears.

Switching Target Parts: If the Concerned Part still won't step aside, make the Concerned Part the new Target Part and work with it as above. Go through all the steps (Steps P2–P5).

Once you have cleared the way, you may decide to return to the original Target Part or continue to work with the new Target Part. This is often a decision for your entire internal system. You may want to stop and ask all the parts you have been working with what is the best way to proceed. Wait a moment for an answer. The truth of what is best for you now will usually emerge.

Sitting on the Sidelines: It is OK for the Concerned Part to watch from the sidelines and step in if it thinks there is danger. If you make this promise to the part, make sure to notice if it returns, acknowledge it, and find out its concerns.

Not Sure if Concerned Part Stepped Aside: If you're not sure whether it stepped aside, proceed with getting to know the Target Part and see what happens. You may later realize that you need to unblend some more or work with this or another Concerned Part.

How to Know That the Concerned Part Hasn't Stepped Aside

1. The Target Part isn't responding to questions, is stonewalling, or can't be accessed. When you ask about its behavior, it says it doesn't trust you.

2. You are using your mind to figure out the Target Part rather than asking it questions.

3. The questions you are asking have a judgmental or accusatory tone.

4. You don't understand why the Target Part is doing what it is doing.

5. You aren't succeeding in developing a trusting relationship with the Target Part.

EXERCISE Mapping Your Parts

Many people find it very helpful to map their parts. Mapping can clarify relationships between parts, flesh out the number of parts at a trailhead, illuminate the protective system, illustrate which parts are central to the system and which are peripheral, show where parts stand in terms of their relationship to the Self, and much more.

Mapping can be done when you are just beginning to get to know your system. You can check in periodically with the original map to see how things have changed as you keep working. You can also use parts mapping as an ongoing tool for visually tracking your internal work and deciding where to focus your attention.

There are many ways to map your system. One way is to use a large sheet of paper and write down the names or images of the parts as you know them. You can draw lines or arrows to illustrate the relationships. Here is my favorite way to map your system:

- Start with a large sheet of newsprint paper.
- Put a heart in the top center and write your name in it. This represents the Self.
- Work with at least two colors of sticky notes. I like to use one color for Protectors and a different color for Exiles. If you have a heart-shaped sticky note for the Self, all the better.

Start by writing the names of parts on sticky notes as you think of them or feel them and put the notes randomly on the paper. If you have a sense that a part is a Protector and another is an Exile, use the appropriate colors. As things become clearer, you can change colors.

Once all the parts are on the paper, sit back and look it over. I recommend doing a centering exercise to get into Self so you can view the parts from that place. If it feels right, take a few deep breaths with your hand on your belly.

Now begin to move the sticky notes to reflect the relationships between the parts.

- Which parts are allied and work together?
- Which parts are polarized and fight each other?
- Which parts hide?
- Which parts protect other parts?
- Which ones are Concerned Parts that would block the Self from getting to know a Target Part?

Once you have rearranged the parts, sit back again and reflect. Have you become aware of any other parts? Add them. Now how does it look and feel?

Notice any shift in your emotional state or body awareness once you have the map in front of you. Do you see a clear entry point where you want to begin your investigation? Do you see parts that need the help and resources of the Self?

Chapter 7

GETTING TO KNOW A PROTECTOR

Normally in therapy, when people work with a part, they either analyze it intellectually or dive into it emotionally. IFS encourages us to do something different from either of those. When using the IFS Model, we stay in Self and make contact with the part from there. We get to know the part by asking it questions and listening to its responses. The part may give us information in the form of words, images, body sensations, emotions, or a sense of direct knowing.

EXERCISE **Getting to Know a Protector**

Choose a Protector Part that you are interested in getting to know. It might be one that is present right now in this moment, or you may access it as described in Chapter 4. See what information is readily available about this Protector: how it feels in your body, what it looks like, and what it says.

On the next page is a list of possible questions to ask the Protector. See which questions are appropriate for this part at this time. You can fill in the part's answers on the page or on a separate piece of paper. There is also space for you to write other questions that flow naturally from your discussion or that feel important to you.

When the part gives an answer that piques your curiosity, follow it up. For example, if the part says, "I want to keep safe," you might ask, "What do you want to keep safe from?" or "Who do you want to keep safe?" Be gentle and don't interrogate the part. Allow time for its answers to unfold naturally and just insert questions to facilitate the process.

Name of the part or role that it serves: _____

> **Naming a Part:** It may be useful to have a name for the part, which could be a descriptive phrase, a person's name, name of a character, or anything else. Make sure the part names itself. The name can change at any time in the future as your understanding of the part evolves.

Questions to help you get to know your part:

What do you do? _____

What is your role in my system? _____

What would you like me to call you?_____

What do you feel? _____

What makes you feel so (feeling)? _____

How do you relate to people? _____

How do you interact with other parts? _____

How do you feel about (an external event or feeling)? _____

What do you want for us? _____

What do you hope to accomplish by (doing your role)? _____

What are you afraid would happen if you didn't (do your role)? _____

_____

What are you afraid we would feel or do if you didn't (do your role)? _____

_____

How long have you been (doing your role)? _____

What caused you to take on this role, and when did you start? _____

How do you feel about your role? _____

What would you like from me? _____

Other question _____

    Answer _____

Other question _____

    Answer _____

Getting a Felt Sense of a Part

This part might not answer your questions with clear, explicit descriptions. Allowing a felt sense of the part or an image of the part to emerge can be particularly important and informative. It's fine if you start out with vague images or body sensings, such as "folded over on itself," "a sense of poignancy," "narrowing in the chest," or "an empty sack." Greet these sensory pieces of information with an open heart and sincere curiosity. Let the part know what you see or feel. For example, "I see that you are collapsed and empty" or "I notice that you're tense and seem anxious." As you stay with the part or ask more questions, the part's unique nature will become clearer. Take your time and don't push for clarity. It will emerge.

Note any subtle images or vague sensations that you notice when getting to know this part.

_____

_____

SAMPLE   **Getting to Know a Protector**

Name of the Part or role that it serves: Angry Part

   When someone unjustly criticizes me, or misinterprets my behavior,

   I get angry and attack them.

Questions to help you get to know your part:

What do you do? Protect you

What is your role in my system? Keep bad people away

What would you like me to call you? The White Knight

What do you feel? Angry, mad, frustrated

What makes you feel so angry? Stupid, heartless, thoughtless people

How do you relate to people? I keep them away.

What do you say? Get out of here!

Sample continued on next page

Sample continued from previous page

How do you interact with other parts? <u>Protect them</u>

How do you feel about this current situation? <u>When other don't take</u> <u>responsibility for their behavior or feelings, I get angry.</u>

What do you want for us? <u>To be safe, happy, and free</u>

What do you hope to accomplish by using anger to protect?
  <u>That we will stay away from bad people</u>

What are you afraid would happen if you didn't use anger to protect?
  <u>We would get hurt.</u>

What are you afraid we would feel or do if you didn't use anger to protect?
  <u>Be friends with the wrong people</u>

How long have you been using anger to protect? <u>Since I was a little girl</u>

What caused you to take on this role, and when did you start?
  <u>Being criticized as a child</u>

How do you feel about your role? <u>I like it, and it's important.</u>

What do you want from me? <u>Love and acknowledgment and appreciation</u>

Chapter 8

DEVELOPING A TRUSTING RELATIONSHIP WITH A PROTECTOR

The protective role that parts take on can be considered extreme. Protector Parts have a narrowly focused view of the world and hold specific beliefs that support their attitudes and behavior. Parts take on extreme roles because they think they have to handle situations on their own. They either don't know that the Self is there, or they don't trust the Self to handle the situation. A major aspect of the goal of IFS is for parts to trust the Self. This may not fully happen until after unburdening, but a good deal of trust can (and needs to) be gained while you are still working with a Protector.

Enhancing Trust

If you take the time to get to know a Protector and it feels understood and appreciated, it will tend to trust you and relax.

Statements that foster trust in the Self:

- I understand why you (do your role).
- I get why you think that is important.
- It makes sense to me (what you do or say or feel).
- I see the pressure that you are under.
- I appreciate your efforts on my behalf.
- I appreciate what you originally did for me.
- I appreciate what you have done for me throughout my life.
- I appreciate what you are doing for me.

Other statements you think of or ones that any of your Protectors specifically want

to hear: _____

EXERCISE   **Developing a Relationship with a Protector**

Choose a Protector to work with. You may decide to choose one that you have been working with, or you may want to choose a new one. Spend as much time as you need to go through Steps P1–P4. Access the part, unblend from the Target Part, and unblend from any Concerned Parts so that you are in Self with the Protector. Here we are getting to know the Protector more deeply and making sure that the Protector can feel your presence as you engage it. Remember to keep checking that you are still in Self during this process.

Protector's name: _____

What it feels: _____

What it looks like: _____

Where it is located in your body: _____

What it says: _____

How it makes you behave: _____

What situations activate it: _____

What Concerned Parts react to it: _____

What its positive intent is: _____

What it is protecting you from: _____

You know quite a bit about the part now. You will probably have noticed a significant shift in your bodily sensations as you went through the above process.

What feels different in this moment as you sit with the part in Self? (Openness in your heart? A sense of rising compassion? A loosening of bodily tension? More space?) Make note of these changes.

_____

_____

> SAMPLE   **Developing a Relationship with a Protector**
>
> Protector's name: <u>Angry Part</u>
>
> What it feels: <u>I don't want to be criticized for who I am. I don't trust</u>
> <u>people to accept me.</u>
>
> What it looks like: <u>A white knight. Strong, shiny, with lots of weapons and</u>
> <u>tools like curses and name calling.</u>
>
> Where it is located in your body: <u>Covering the chest area. Tension in my</u>
> <u>shoulders.</u>
>
> What it says: <u>Get away from me, stupid people. Take responsibility for</u>
> <u>yourself. Get away from me.</u>
>
> How it makes you behave: <u>Cursing and yelling</u>
>
> What situations activate it: <u>When people are mean or criticizing</u>
>
> What Concerned Parts react to it: <u>Ashamed, frightened</u>
>
> What its positive intent is: <u>Wants me to be myself and to be around people</u>
> <u>who will accept me</u>
>
> What it is protecting you from: <u>Trying to protect me from bad people who</u>
> <u>are unsafe</u>

Appreciating Parts

When you appreciate a part, you focus on its positive aspects, not necessarily its behavior. You can understand the part's motivation and its positive intent for you. You can have compassion for the job that it tried to do and how hard it worked to protect you from the danger it perceived. Sometimes it's hard to "appreciate" a part that has given you a hard time. Inner Critics, for example, often say terrible things to us to protect us from possible failure, danger, or the judgment of others. When you are in Self, you can let the part know, "I get you. I see what you have been trying to do for me. I understand the rationale behind your behavior. I see how hard you have been working for me and how you have often had to go it alone in taking care of me."

What do you understand or appreciate about your Protector?

_____

_____

_____

_____

Let the part know what you see or understand. You might tell it in words what you appreciate about it and what you see that it has been trying to do for you. You might let it know you understand how hard it has been working, how lonely it has been, and what it has been up against. You might just open your heart and let flow a fountain of gratitude for its efforts and its situation.

How does the Protective Part respond to your understanding and appreciation?

_____

_____

_____

Helping a Protector to Relax in Real Time

Once you have gotten to know a part and developed a trusting relationship with it, you are likely to be able to work with it whenever it arises in real time in your life. Here is a way to do this that may help it relax and allow you to lead from Self.

When you notice that a part is activated at some point during your day, access it briefly and see if you are blended with it. Often, you are. The part is blended with you because some situation in your life has come up that frightens the part and makes it believe that it must take over. When you become aware of the part, take a moment to get in Self. From this place, acknowledge the part and ask it to relax and allow you to lead from Self. You may want to promise that you will spend some time with it later to deal with its concerns.

EXERCISE   Helping a Protector to Relax in Real Time

Think of a situation in which a Protector gets triggered that causes you to behave in

a problematic way. _____

Following Steps P1–P5, do a session with yourself or with a partner in which you get to know the Protector that is causing the difficulty. Use the questions below to help you get to know the Protector and begin to form a trusting relationship with it.

Name of Protector: _____

Situation(s) that activate this Protector: _____

How it behaves: _____

If you were able to act from Self, how would you like to behave in that situation?

_____

Do you have the life skills necessary to accomplish the positive behavior you are aiming for? _____

_____

If not, what kind of support would you need to be able to act in the way you desire?

_____

Once you have unblended from the Protector and your Concerned Parts, and you are in contact with the Protector from Self, ask if it will let you lead the next time you are in a similar situation.

What is its response? _____

On the next page, list the Protector's concerns and your thinking **from Self** about how to handle them.

Concern: _____

Response: _____

Potential support: _____

Concern: _____

Response: _____

Potential support: _____

Concern: _____

Response: _____

Potential support: _____

Think about when this situation is likely to occur over the next few weeks.

_____

Set an intention to be aware of whether this Protector takes over at those times. When it does, work with it as described above to help it relax and let you lead. If this works, take notes on what happened as soon as you can.

What did your behavior look like when you were leading from Self? _____

_____

What were the results? _____

_____

Continue to track this kind of situation over the next few weeks, doing this exercise each time the part is activated. Each evening before you go to bed, review the day to see if the situation arose, and take notes (or expand your notes) on what happened when you did this exercise. If the Protector allowed you to lead and things turned out well, check to see if it now trusts you more. If you didn't notice the situation at the time or you didn't do the exercise, explore what got in the way. If this is a situation that doesn't come up very often, it wouldn't make sense to do this review every night. You might decide to review once a week. Choose whatever time frame is appropriate.

Day	Situation	Protector	Self-Led Behavior	Part's Response

S A M P L E   **Helping a Protector to Relax in Real Time**

Name of Protector: <u>The Distractor</u>

Situation(s) that activate this Protector: <u>Loss</u>

How it behaves: <u>Tries to distract with activities or fantasies</u>

If you were able to act from Self, how would you like to behave in that

   situation? <u>Feel my feelings a little at a time</u>

Do you have the life skills necessary to pull off the positive behavior you are

   aiming for? <u>Yes, I have self-compassion and faith.</u>

If not, what kind of support would you need to be able to act in the way you

   desire? <u>Help from friends and loved ones — people who understand</u>

Sample continued on next page

Sample continued from previous page

Once you have unblended from the Protector and your Concerned Parts, and you are in contact with the Protector from Self, ask if it will let you lead the next time you are in a similar situation.

What is its response? <u>No</u>

Protector's concerns and your thinking FROM SELF about how to handle them.

Concern: <u>You won't be able to handle the feelings.</u>

Response: <u>We can feel them a little bit at a time.</u>

Potential support: <u>Therapist, friends, family</u>

Concern: <u>Doesn't have any tools or resources</u>

Response: <u>Yes, we do. We have patience, intuition, good ideas, and the ability to explore and research.</u>

Potential support: <u>Lots of smart friends</u>

Concern: <u>We don't have anyone.</u>

Response: <u>Yes, we do have friends and the ability to meet new people.</u>

Potential support: <u>The people I love and trust</u>

Think about when this situation is likely to occur over the next few weeks.

<u>A good friend is going on extended travel abroad</u>

What did your behavior look like when you were leading from Self?

<u>Stop and be aware of the feelings. Let myself recognize and feel the feelings. Let myself reach out and receive help, love, and support from friends. Come up with solutions. Envision positive change.</u>

What were the results? <u>Living more in the present moment. Being more engaged in life.</u>

Chapter 9

WHEN A PROTECTOR DOESN'T TRUST YOU

Every Protector has its own unique history that is made up of experiences with both the outside world and the inside world. These experiences result in a set of beliefs and expectations. In general, Protectors have not dealt with Self directly, as we are trying to do here. Protectors often have good reason to be cautious and careful. They are trying to prevent reinjury or a repeat of past disappointments. It's important to be respectful of these cautions and deal openly with a Protector to gain its trust.

You will know that a Protector doesn't trust you if it is not responsive to your questions or other efforts to get to know it. You might feel as though it is being uncooperative or have a sense that it is turning away from you or tuning you out. A Concerned Part may arise that starts to doubt the process or criticize you.

- If a Protector isn't answering questions or is otherwise not cooperating:
    - ➤ Ask the part if it is aware of you. Can it feel you here, trying to make contact with it and get to know it?
    - ➤ Ask the part directly if it trusts you. Does it feel that your efforts are sincere and well meaning?

- If the part lets you know that it doesn't trust you:
    - ➤ Check to see if you are really in Self or whether a subtle Concerned Part has gotten in the way. The Target Part may be sensing one or more Concerned Parts and not trust you because of that. If that's the case, unblend from the Concerned Part(s) and try to make contact again.
    - ➤ If you are in Self, ask the part why it doesn't trust you. Assume that something in your history has caused its concerns about your awareness of it or your capacity to take care of it. If that's the case, reassure the part as much as possible about who you are today. It may be useful to explain that you didn't have

much access to Self when you were younger but that you've learned how to reliably access Self since then, so you can now be counted on as a supportive resource.

Sometimes a part needs more time. You might have an Impatient Part that's trying to rush the process. You might have a Pleaser Part that's trying to appease someone else by pushing this work along, or you may have a part that has an outside goal about the resolution of this issue. Parts can be very sensitive to these subtle pressures. They may have been created in situations in which trust was an important factor. So as you tease out the possible underlying parts that are creating the distrust, be sure to view them with compassion. They are Protectors, too, and are invested in their owns goals for your system. Ask for their cooperation in the larger effort to heal the system and create wholeness.

- If the part is still hesitant to trust:
  - ➤ Ask it what happened in the past to make it not trust people. Again, listen from Self. Being with the part in a compassionate way often allows it to take in your sincerity. As you do your best to reassure the part about its fears, remind it that you are here in Self today and that this is not the same as the past.
  - ➤ Remember that if a persistent Concerned Part keeps asserting itself into the process, it may be appropriate to make that part a new Target Part.

Note here any history that may be affecting your part's ability to trust you at this time.

_____

_____

_____

(See page 32 for parts' typical fears.)

If you are working with a distrustful part, note on the next page any fears or concerns that your distrustful part has as well as the answers that feel appropriate to you at this time.

Fear: _____

Your response: _____

_____

Part's response: _____

_____

Fear: _____

Your response: _____

_____

Part's response: _____

_____

Fear: _____

Your response: _____

_____

Part's response: _____

_____

Chapter 10

SESSION BASICS

Starting a New IFS Session

Whenever you begin a new session, it is a good idea to start by checking in with the part you focused on in the previous session. Access the Target Part from the previous session. You may need to repeat some of the questions about getting to know the part in order to fully establish it in your consciousness and connect with it. If the part was still in process during the previous session, it is usually best to continue working with that part in the new session until you finish unburdening it (unless something urgent has come up in the meantime). Access the part and continue from the step you ended with in the previous session unless any new Protectors get in the way. If that happens, work with those Protectors first.

Triggered Parts

A part can be triggered during any exploration. Even though you have gone through the process to become centered in Self, a part may arise and take over the seat of consciousness without you realizing it.

Here are some signals that a part has taken over:

- You speak **as** the part rather than reporting on what the part says to you.
- You get lost in telling the story of what happened, and it triggers a part.
- You begin to see the world from the viewpoint of the part or you are caught up in its beliefs.
- You get more and more charged up with the part's feelings.

Awareness is the key. The trick to finding your way back to a centered and grounded place is detecting that you are blended. When you become aware that you have lost your compassionate or curious perspective, you can work more effectively on unblending and returning to Self.

If you are working with a partner, you can give that person permission to point out to you when you are blended with a part. If you are working with a part in real time—that is, in a life situation—you can sense the shift in your body when you're blended with a part versus speaking and acting from Self.

Speaking *For* a Part Versus Speaking *As* a Part

The skills and understanding that we learn in IFS are particularly valuable in our interactions with others. Whether we are talking to business associates, friends, or intimates, parts language can clarify feelings and intentions, ease tensions, and create an atmosphere of open communication and respect.

Generally it is advisable to speak **for** a part (from Self) rather than speaking **as** the part. For example, if the part is angry, instead of saying, "I am angry," you can say, "There's a part of me that's angry."

When you speak for a part, you are more likely to be responsible for the part's feelings and issues rather than blaming others for them. You're less likely to say things that will hurt other people's Exiles and therefore trigger their angry Protectors. Speaking for a part is particularly useful when you're talking with someone about a touchy emotional issue between you or when you're trying to resolve a conflict with someone. This is especially helpful in intimate relationships (see Chapter 21). It is also advisable when working on conflicts in groups. It's a simple rule that helps you engage in true dialogue.

EXERCISE   Speaking for Parts

Think of a situation in which parts of you are activated—possibly a conversation with another person. Note which parts are present and explore the difference between speaking **as** a part and speaking **for** the part.

Situation	Part	Part's Feeling: Speaking AS the Part	From Self: Speaking FOR the Part

Situation	Part	Part's Feeling: Speaking AS the Part	From Self: Speaking FOR the Part

What difference do you notice in your body and your feelings when you speak

as the part versus **for** the part? _____

_____

_____

SAMPLE   **Speaking for Parts**

Situation	Part	Part's Feeling: Speaking AS the Part	From Self: Speaking FOR the Part
A friend doesn't show up for a lunch date	Worried	What the heck happened to you? I was worried sick that you were in a car accident.	When you didn't show up, a part of me was really worried that something happened to you.
	Disappointed	Where were you? I was really looking forward to being with you. I thought you were coming. Don't I mean anything to you?	When you didn't show up, I was disappointed, and a part of me felt like I didn't mean anything to you.
	Angry	You are so selfish. Didn't you know I was waiting for you? You don't think of anyone but yourself. Get it together. You can't even show up for your friends.	A part of me was so mad at you when you didn't show up.
	Judgmental	You're such a loser, you can't even show up when you say you will.	I know that a part of me can be very judgmental, and it was hard to control it when you didn't show up as promised.

Parts Detection

When you are getting to know a Protector, a part may become activated and need to be worked with. There are a number of possibilities:

1. A Concerned Part is blended with you in a way that disrupts the process. Here are some examples (see Chapter 6):

- You're figuring out the part or describing it rather than asking questions and listening for its responses (a Thinker or an Administrator Part).

- You feel angry at the Target Part (an Angry Part has been activated).

- You feel as though you want to stop the work (an Avoidant Part).

- You become more and more intellectual in your approach to the work (an Intellectualizer or an Achiever Part).

- You space out (a Foggy Part or a Dissociator).

- You get blocked emotionally (an Avoidant Part or another Protector).

- You start thinking about other things (a Distractor Part).

The trick is detecting the part—becoming aware that something is disrupting your IFS process and then realizing it means that a Concerned Part has been activated and is blended with you.

Once you become aware that a part has arisen, you focus on that part and find out what it is doing and why. You are especially interested in finding out what it is afraid of that made it disrupt your process. A good question is, "What are you afraid would happen if you weren't doing your job right now?"

When you have gotten to know the part and have established some trust, you can ask it to relax, step aside, and allow you to continue your work. However, you may need to switch your focus, make this part the Target Part, and work with it further.

2. An Exile is activated. This is usually the Exile that is being protected by the Target Protector. The trick is to realize that it is a different part from the Target Part, which may not be obvious. For example, you're getting to know a part that tends to avoid doing certain things in your life, and you feel the shame that it is trying not to feel. This is probably the Exile that the Protector is trying to avoid. It is usually a good idea to acknowledge the Exile and then ask it to wait. You can explain to it that you will be coming to heal it, but first you must get to know the Protector and get its permission (see Chapter 11).

3. A polarized part—another Protector—is activated that is polarized with the Target Protector. For example, you're working with a part that avoids things in your life, and a part pops up that really wants to get those things done. See Chapter 22 on polarization for how to work with this type of situation.

4. Another Protector is activated that protects the same Exile that is being protected by the Target Protector. For example, a part comes up that is skeptical about inner work, and this part is trying to protect against the same shame Exile that the Avoidant Part is protecting. Ask the second Protector to step aside until you have finished working with the Target Protector (the Avoidant Part). You may need to reassure it that you won't contact the Exile (shame) until you have its permission. When you finish getting to know the Target Protector, do the same work with this second one. Get permission from both of them before you get to know the Exile.

EXERCISE Detecting a Part That Has Taken Over

Think of a situation in which you were working with one part and became aware that another part had taken over.

Part you were working with: _____

Part that took over: _____

What type of part was it?

_____ Concerned

_____ Exile

_____ Polarized Part

_____ Protector

Part's motivation: _____

Part's fears: _____

How you worked with the part: _____

WORKING WITH EXILES

Step 2. Getting Permission to Work with an Exile

Step 3. Getting to Know an Exile

    E1. Accessing an Exile

    E2. Unblending from an Exile

    E3. Unblending from Concerned Parts

    E4. Finding Out About an Exile

    E5. Developing a Trusting Relationship with an Exile

Step 4. Accessing and Witnessing Childhood Origins

Step 5. Reparenting an Exile

Step 6: Retrieving an Exile

Step 7. Unburdening an Exile

Step 8. Integration and Unburdening
       a Protector

❶ Exile hidden away

❷ Protector protects Exile
by blocking access to it

❸ Protector grants permission
for Self to get to know Exile

Chapter 11

GETTING PERMISSION TO WORK WITH AN EXILE

Exiles are parts that hold pain. They are usually, but not necessarily, young parts. Because it was not acceptable to feel or experience the discomfort they had in childhood or during times of trauma, they have been exiled from ordinary consciousness. Protectors developed to keep Exiles out of consciousness so we could function in everyday life.

Principles

Whenever there is a Protector, there is always one or more Exiles that it is protecting. One of the key IFS principles is that you never work with an Exile until you have permission from all the Protectors who have concerns about it. It's important to get permission from Protectors so they support access to the Exile. Otherwise, they'll continue to feel protective and will work hard to block access.

It is best to make sure you have a trusting relationship with the Protector before you ask permission to get to know the Exile. Asking permission for access to an Exile is a big interruption to the system of protection that has likely been in place for a long time. It is not to be taken lightly.

Review Steps P1–P5 of working with Protectors (Chapters 7–9) before asking permission to work with an Exile.

When You Have Permission to Make Contact with the Exile

When the Protector has granted you permission to make contact with the Exile, you may become aware of a number of subtle or not-so-subtle shifts in your consciousness. Here are just some of the possibilities:

- You may become aware of an Exile by feeling it or hearing its voice. In some cases, you may think it is still the Protector, but it may be the Exile surfacing.
- You may become aware of which Exile is being protected, especially when the Protector tells you what it is afraid would happen if it didn't do its role. For example, the Protector might say, "I'm afraid that you will be flooded with sadness."
- You may have an image of the Exile behind or below the Protector or in a far-off corner of your mind.
- You may experience vague or intense sensations such as a smell, a taste, a bodily tension, or an image of a scene.
- You may have a memory of a time, a place, or an incident that was significant in childhood.

You might also ask the Protector to show you the part it is protecting.

EXERCISE   Making Initial Contact with an Exile

For the exercises in the next chapters, you may either continue the work you have been doing with the Protector you were working with earlier or begin a new piece of work by accessing a Protector you are curious about now. Remember to go through all of the Steps P1–P5 in working with a new Protector: accessing it, unblending from it, unblending from Concerned Parts, and getting to know and developing a relationship with the Protector so you have permission to work with the Exile.

If you are continuing your work with the Protector from the previous exercises, take some quiet moments to go inside, ground yourself by focusing on your breath, and feel yourself being supported by whatever you are sitting or lying on. Reconnect with the Protector and make sure it remembers who you are before you begin to make contact with the Exile.

Protector: _____

Positive intent: _____

What the Protector feared would happen if it didn't play its role:

_____

Protected Exile: _____

How you know that the Exile that has been protected is available:

_____

    You may ask the Protector directly for permission to get to know the Exile. After you get permission, it may be a good idea to check to see if there are any other Protectors that object to your contacting the Exile.

Other Protectors that come up around this Exile:

_____

    If the Protector doesn't give permission, ask what its concerns are or what it is afraid would happen if you contacted the Exile.

Fears or concerns that this Protector has about contacting the Exile:

_____

_____

SAMPLE   **Making Initial Contact with an Exile**

Protector: <u>Angry Protector</u>

Positive intent: <u>Wants to be accepted by others</u>

What the Protector feared would happen if it didn't play its role: <u>She would be around people who would be mean to her and criticize her.</u>

Exile: <u>The Good Girl</u>

How you know that the Exile that has been protected is available: <u>I have an image of a sad little girl about age 7.</u>

Other Protectors: <u>An Inner Critic that looks like the nun in the new school I attended.</u>

Common Protector Fears and How to Deal with Them

Remember that it is important to stay in Self when responding to a Protector's fear and concerns. It is helpful to repeat and validate its concerns before answering.

Fear: The Exile has too much pain, or it is a black hole of chaos and overwhelm.
Response: Explain that you will stay in Self and get to know the Exile. Assure it that you will move slowly, step-by-step, and not just dive into its pain.

Fear: There isn't any point in going into the pain. The Exile can't change. The past is the past.
Response: Explain that it is possible to heal the Exile. IFS knows how to do that.

Fear: The Protector will no longer have a role and therefore will be eliminated or lose power.
Response: Explain that the Protector can choose a new role in your psyche.

Fear: The Protector doesn't trust you.
Response: Ask why and work on that issue with the Protector.

While working with an Exile, it is common for a Protector to pop up. Use your parts detector to recognize if this happens. Notice if your feeling state or body energy changes. If you are working with someone else, notice any changes in tone of voice or physical movements.

If the Protector that arises is the one you were already working with, ask what its concern is and why it still doesn't want to give permission. Work with it until it is comfortable again.

If it is a new Protector, spend some time getting to know it and then ask for permission to work with the Exile.

How did you handle your Protector's fears or concerns? What did it need to hear from you?

_____

_____

Chapter 12

UNBLENDING FROM AN EXILE

Exiles

Exiles have two motivations: They want to be heard, and they want to be healed. The only hope they have of being healed is to get your attention. The main way they try to communicate their feelings is by letting them out and possibly flooding you. When an Exile is blended, its feelings and bodily experiences may feel frightening and overwhelming. Keep in mind that an Exile may not share with you all its information or story at one time.

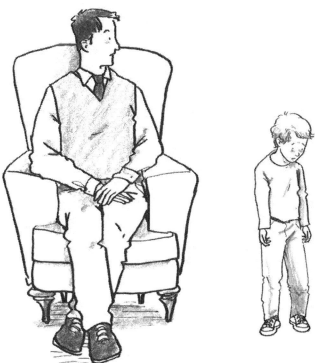

Protectors

Protectors have three main motivations:

- To keep Exiles safe from reinjury
- To contain Exiles' feelings so you can function
- To keep Exiles from acting out in infantile ways that either put them in danger or expose the system to vulnerability or shame

Every Protector is motivated by the energy of an Exile. The stronger and more vigilant a Protector is, the more traumatized and vulnerable the Exile probably is.

Self

Self is the place of consciousness where you can see all parts with compassion and be genuinely curious about who they are and what has happened to cause their pain and suffering. Once you have gone through the previous step (Chapter 11, Getting Permission to Work with an Exile) and are in contact with the Exile, **you** are in a unique position to be of service to it. The key, as always, is to be in Self.

From Self, you can witness the Exile's story. If the Exile were a lake, instead of diving into the lake, you would calmly sit beside it and look in the water.

How to Work with an Exile to Help It Unblend

Exiles can get very excited to have your attention and finally have an opportunity to be heard. They often want to blend with you and let you know everything they feel. They need to be gently helped to trust that you are there and willing to listen and to understand that you can listen better if you are separate.

When the door to the past or a trauma has been opened, many Exiles will often try to crowd through the door at the same time so they can be heard. They need to be reassured that you will get to each of them in turn. Decide who you want to work with first, and ask the others to wait. Usually just being acknowledged and promised some attention will quiet things down.

Reasons for Needing to Be Separate from an Exile
- To protect yourself from being flooded with too much pain
- To keep Protectors from being triggered
- To allow you to be present to witness the Exile's pain and story
- So you can be an agent of healing for the Exile
- So you can facilitate your work successfully

Guidelines for Working with Exiles

Exile work is often more easily done with a partner who can witness your experience and support you in staying in Self with the Exile. (See Chapter 20 for information on working with a partner). If you are working alone, create as supportive an environment as possible. Make sure you are in a safe, quiet space. Take some time to center and ground yourself before you begin. Use the journal tools below to keep track of your experience. Seek outside support, if you can, to process your experience, perhaps a trusted friend or a professional. Follow up with the Exile between sessions if you take breaks between any of the last stages of the process.

EXERCISE   Unblending from an Exile

For this exercise, you can either continue the work you have been doing with the Exile you were previously getting to know or begin a new piece of work. If you begin a new piece of work, make sure to complete the previous steps, up to making contact with the Exile.

If you are continuing your work with the Exile from the previous exercise, take some quiet moments to go inside, ground yourself by focusing on your breath, and feel yourself being supported by whatever you are sitting or lying on. Reconnect with the Protector and make sure it remembers who you are before beginning to make contact with the Exile.

If necessary, focus on unblending from this Exile. Fill in your notes on this process below.

How do you know that the Exile is here? (an image, a sensation, a memory, etc.)

_____

If you feel yourself emotionally charged, physically agitated, contracted, or depressed, you are probably blended with the Exile. If so, ask it to unblend from you.

What is the name of the Exile you are working with?   _____

Let the Exile know that you are aware that it is blended with you and you are feeling its feelings. Sometimes just this recognition calms things down a little.

Check off below any of the unblending procedures that have been helpful in working with this Exile.

Ways to Unblend

_____ Consciously separate from the Exile and return to Self.

_____ Ask the Exile to contain its feelings so you can be there for it.

_____ Ask the Exile to not overwhelm you if you move closer to it.

_____ Do a centering/grounding induction to bring yourself back to Self.

Use the journal space below to take specific notes on this process.

_____

_____

If the Exile won't contain its feelings, ask it why it doesn't want to.

_____

_____

What the Exile is concerned about that is making it reluctant to unblend:

_____

_____

Exiles are often afraid that they won't be heard or that they will be exiled again, for example, pushed away out of consciousness, restricted, or forgotten.

Explain to the Exile that if it contains its feelings, you can safely be there for it. Explain that you really want to hear its feelings and witness what happened to it, but you need to be separate to do that.

What helps this Exile unblend:

_____

_____

Blending During Exile Work

Once you start working with an Exile, blending can happen at any time. This usually takes the form of feeling too much of the Exile's pain. Be aware of blending so you can unblend (come back to Self) as soon as you notice it. If blending is a problem, don't speak in first person as the Exile. You might speak to it out loud, for example: "I hear that you were very frightened during that incident in your childhood. I'm here, and I'm willing to listen to you."

Conscious Blending

Sometimes it is OK to agree to feel the Exile's pain. If you are solidly in Self, you may be able to allow the Exile to show you its pain by having you feel it. This is fine as long as you remain centered and able to be present for the Exile from Self. You can even feel the pain fully and express it as long as you are in Self while this is happening. Look at the five reasons for being separate on page 76. If they are all true while you are feeling the Exile's pain, you are still in Self, so it is OK to proceed.

Use the journal space below to take specific notes on this process.

Protector Resurgence During the Unblending Process

Very often when you are in the process of getting to know an Exile, unblending from it, and witnessing it (Chapters 12–14), Protectors that have agreed to step aside will reassert themselves. You might suddenly feel angry at what happened and be full of attacking rage, or you might get foggy or feel dissociated. When you notice any of these situations, acknowledge that the Protector is there. If you have an agreement with this Protector, remind it what it promised you. If it won't relax, you may have to do some work with it again at this time.

If a new Protector asserts itself, you may have to spend some time with it before it will relax and grant you access to the Exile again.

Use the journal space below to take specific notes on this process.

_____

_____

_____

_____

Chapter 13

GETTING TO KNOW AN EXILE

The process of getting to know an Exile is similar to working with a Protector: accessing the Exile, unblending from it, checking for Concerned Parts, unblending from Concerned Parts, finding out about the Exile, and developing a trusting relationship with it.

The Difference: Concerned Parts have different concerns about allowing you to get to know an Exile versus a Protector.

Concerned Parts' Fears About Unblending from an Exile

Fear: Concerned Parts may be afraid of the Exile taking over or your getting overwhelmed by the Exile's pain.

Response: Explain that you will stay in Self and not give the Exile power.

Fear: Concerned Parts may not think they or you can take care of the Exile because you don't have the capacity or because the Exile's needs are too great.

Response: Explain that: (a) in Self, you have an unlimited capacity for caring and compassion, (b) an Exile doesn't need a lot of real-time attention and energy, even if it can feel that way, and (c) in Self, it feels like a joy, not a burden, to care for an Exile.

Sometimes there are signs that the protective system is not ready for you to work alone with an Exile. You may need to work with a partner (see Chapter 20) or with a trained therapist. One way you'll know is if you have consistent difficulty accessing or remaining in Self, for example, if a Protector is so strong that you end up falling asleep, getting distracted, or engaging in some form of compulsive behavior every time you try to do the work. It is also advisable to work with another person if you know that this Exile holds trauma that you have never processed (abuse, death of a loved one, witnessing or being involved in an accident or natural disaster, and so on).

EXERCISE   **Getting to Know an Exile**

Choose an Exile that you would like to get to know. You can either continue to work with the Exile you were previously getting to know or begin a new piece of work starting with a Protector, unblending from the Protector, asking Concerned Parts to relax, and working through the process of identifying and making contact with the Exile.

Wherever you choose to start, begin by taking a few moments to bring yourself into your body. Make sure you are supported, either feeling your feet on the floor or sensing the support of the chair you are sitting on. Focus on your breath. Notice whether it is fast or slow, deep or shallow, high in your chest or low in your belly. Allow your breath to deepen as you invite your body to relax, and reassure your Protectors that **you** are there and are interested in getting to know the Exile.

From this place, make contact with the Exile.

Now check for any Concerned Parts. Do so by asking, "How do I feel toward this Exile right now?"

Note below any Concerned Parts that you discover.

Ask each part what fears it has about the Exile it is protecting.

Concerned Part: _____

Fears: _____

Your response _____

Part's response _____

Concerned Part: _____

Fears: _____

Your response _____

Part's response _____

Concerned Part: _____

Fears: _____

Your response _____

Part's response _____

When the Concerned Parts have relaxed and the Exile is available for contact, what do you notice?

What it looks like: _____

What it feels in its body: _____

Where it is: _____

How close it is to you: _____

Whether it knows you are there: _____

Whether it knows who you are: _____

As you begin to make contact with the Exile, let it know that you are here and are interested in getting to know it. How do you do that?

_____ Speak to it

_____ Step closer to it

_____ Open your heart to it

_____ Breathe with it by synchronizing your breath with its breath

_____ Look it in the eye

_____ Make physical contact with it

_____ Other ways _____

_____

_____

Finding Out About an Exile

You will notice that many of these questions are similar to the ones we asked Protectors. We make sure to ask about the Exile's age and when it was created. Also note that Exile parts can be layered by ages. Sometimes a part is an Exile and a Protector at the same time, for example, a six-year-old that holds its own pain and also protects a younger Exile.

EXERCISE   Finding Out About an Exile

Name of the Exile: _____

> **Exile Names:** Exiles often have names that are related to the age or time they were created. Make sure each Exile names itself. The name can change at any time in the future as your understanding of the part evolves.

Possible questions to help you get to know your Exile:

Remember to ask these questions with great care and an open heart. Follow the thread of the conversation as you would with anyone who is delicate and cautious.

Who are you? _____

What do you do? _____

_____

What is your role in my system? _____

_____

What would you like me to call you? _____

When were you born? _____

How old are you? _____

What do you feel? _____

What makes you feel so (feeling)? _____

_____

The sample exercises for Chapters 11–18 reflect a single piece of work with an Exile. They follow the course of a session in which the client got to know an Exile, witnessed its story, and reparented and unburdened it.

SAMPLE   **Finding Out About an Exile**

Name of the Exile: <u>Little girl</u>

Who are you? <u>A sad child</u>

What do you do? <u>Cry and cower in a corner</u>

What is your role in my system? <u>I hold the pain of being criticized and rejected.</u>

What would you like me to call you? <u>The good girl</u>

When were you born? <u>Catholic school, second grade</u>

How old are you? <u>Seven years old</u>

What do you feel? <u>Lonely</u>

What makes you feel so lonely? <u>No one will play with me. I don't have any friends. People call me weird.</u>

How do you relate to people outside? <u>I try to be friends with people, and they reject me.</u>

How do you interact with other parts? <u>I have angry parts that help protect me.</u>

How do you feel about the current situation? <u>I got hurt by an adult friend.</u>

Other questions you have for this part:

What kind of friends do you want?

Answer: <u>Friends who will help me feel good about myself</u>

Can you tell me more about this kind of friend?

Answer: <u>They would be playful, fun, trustworthy, kind, and, most important, would like me.</u>

Checking with the Exile

Frequently check to see how you are feeling toward the Exile. Take time to make sure you stay in Self and keep a compassionate heart available. It is easy to get triggered by an Exile. Their stories can make us angry for them. Their fears can sometimes make them feel elusive or frustrating. Remember, this is a new relationship. You want to stay present and open so it can develop. Notice how the Exile's responses to you are affecting your feelings toward it.

EXERCISE   **Noticing an Exile in Real Time**

Now take an opportunity to notice when an Exile is activated in real time. Each time you are in one of these situations, pay careful attention to see if the Exile is triggered. If it is, what does it feel? Note how you are aware that a part is there. Do you notice physical shifts, behavioral changes, emotional flows? Does a Protector become activated to guard against this Exile? If so, how does it act?

Date	Situation	Awareness	Parts Triggered	Feelings	Behavior

SAMPLE   **Noticing an Exile in Real Time**

Exile: <u>Little Anthony</u>

Situations: <u>My wife criticizes my eating habits; not taking care of myself.</u>

Date	Situation	Awareness	Parts Triggered	Feelings	Behavior
Mon.	Wife asks what I had for lunch. Pizza? Fries?	Sinking in chest Fists clench, turn red and steamy	Inadequate failure (Little Anthony) Protective anger	Feel small and powerless Guilty Angry	Withdraw, then get angry
Wed.	Boss asks if my part of presentation is ready.	Sinking in chest Nervousness	Inadequate failure The good boy	Frightened, small Guilty Scared	Hesitate, stutter, consider lying Running around getting things done
Fri.	Out to dinner with wife. She's telling me what to order.	Sinking in chest I take a deep breath.	Bad boy Some sense of Self	Bad, guilty, as if I'm a disappointment Sense of expansion and settling	At first withdrawing and then making a decision to speak up for myself

Chapter 14

ACCESSING & WITNESSING CHILDHOOD ORIGINS

Once you have gotten to know an Exile and developed some trust with it, you can access the childhood origins of its pain. In IFS, the memories, intense feelings, somatic experiences, beliefs, and confusions that Exiles hold are referred to as *burdens.* They are what the Exile has experienced or taken on. The burdens are not intrinsic to the Exile, which is why they can be released. From the IFS perspective, the Exile itself wasn't created by painful experiences—the burdens were.

Witnessing the Exile's Story

As mentioned earlier, Exiles primarily want to be heard. For the most part, we can assume that they didn't have someone present during the childhood situation to accurately mirror their feelings, adequately protect them, offer solace or comfort, or put into perspective what they were experiencing. A major role of Self is to provide this witnessing function.

Sometimes when an Exile shows up, you spontaneously know the story it holds. The Exile comes as a child with a memory from your past. You see and remember the situation, and you know what happened and the burden that the Exile holds.

Other times, as you meet and begin to gain the trust of

an Exile, you may have to ask it to show you the origins of its burdens. The following are a few good prompts to encourage an Exile to tell you its story:

- Please show me an image or a memory of when you learned to feel this way.
- Please show me a time when you first took on this role in childhood.
- What do you want me to know about you that would help me understand you better?

Images and Memories

Memories can come in many forms. They can be visual stories, like watching a movie of the event, or they can be physical cues that remind you of an earlier time. They can be body memories, such as pain, tension, sounds, or smells that eventually lead to more information. They can be emotional feelings that flow through you with or without actual content. It is not important that the part show you a conscious memory of a specific incident. *It is important that you consciously stay with the part in Self as the memory sequence unfolds.*

Memories may not be clear or sequential for these reasons:

1. The memory might be preverbal because it happened when you were too young to have conscious memory or an understanding of what was taking place. This is called *implicit memory.* It comes in the form of a body or emotional sensing or an image that doesn't correspond to any conscious memory or story about yourself that you're aware of.

2. The memory might not be one incident but rather a particular family interaction that happened hundreds or thousands of times. In this case, there might be one conscious memory that represents all of these, or there might be an image or other less clear sensing that represents them all.

3. The memory might not be available in conscious form, but it will show up as an image or other form of implicit memory such as body sensations.

Once the Exile shows you an image or memory, ask it to fill in the details as much as it wants to. Be especially interested in what happened and how this made the part feel. You are there as a compassionate, caring witness. It is fine if the part shows you a series of memories that are all related to one feeling or issue. However, when you move on to the next steps, it is best to focus on one of these memories at a time.

Before you move on to the next steps, make sure the part has shown you everything it wants to and that it feels that you understand how bad the experience was.

EXERCISE   Accessing and Witnessing a Childhood Memory

This exercise involves working with a childhood memory. You'll be spending some time with an Exile, witnessing its story and finding out the impact of these events on it.

You can either continue the work that you have been doing with the Exile you were previously getting to know or begin a new piece of work. If you choose to explore a new Exile, begin with the Protector and go through Steps P1–P5 until you have made contact with and developed a safe relationship with the Exile.

Wherever you choose to start, begin by taking a few moments to activate Self energy. You might have a habitual way to do this, or you might take a few deep breaths, relax your shoulders, wiggle your jaw, and sink deeply into your body.

With another deep breath, let your Protectors know that **you**, in Self, are here and are interested in hearing this Exile's story.

Name of Exile: _____

As you got to know the Exile, did it come with a clear memory? _____

_____

Did you need to ask it to reveal its childhood story? _____

If so, what questions were helpful? _____

_____

Were you aware of other Protectors coming in to protect the Exile during the witnessing process? If so, who showed up? _____

_____

What were the Exile's feelings and beliefs? _____

_____

_____

What happened in childhood? _____

_____

_____

_____

_____

How did that make the Exile feel? _____

_____

_____

How do you (in Self) feel toward the Exile now? _____

_____

Does the Exile feel that you understand how bad it was? _____

_____

Use the journal space below for other notes on the witnessing process.

_____

_____

_____

_____

S A M P L E   **Accessing and Witnessing a Childhood Memory**

Name of Exile: <u>The Good Girl</u>

As you got to know the Exile, did it come with a clear memory? <u>Yes</u>

Did you need to ask it to reveal its childhood story? <u>No. When I appreciated the Protector, the story just came into my consciousness. I remembered what it was like before the Protector was there when other kids made fun of me.</u>

If so, what questions were helpful? <u>Can you appreciate how the Protector feels that her job is necessary?</u>

Were you aware of other Protectors coming in to protect the child during the witnessing process? <u>Yes.</u>

If so, who showed up? <u>The Inner Critic showed up in the form of a nun.</u>

Exile's feelings and beliefs: <u>I am weird and strange, and something is wrong with me.</u>

What happened in childhood? <u>The nun told me that something was wrong with me and that's why I didn't have friends.</u>

How did that make the Exile feel? <u>Lonely, weird, and rejected</u>

How do you (in Self) feel toward the Exile now? <u>Compassionate and caring</u>

Does the Exile feel that you understand how bad it was? <u>Yes, it can feel me here caring for it. It relaxes and can sit still.</u>

Chapter 15

REPARENTING AN EXILE

Once you have accessed and witnessed the childhood origins of an Exile's pain, you can reparent the Exile. This means you provide healing to the Exile by supplying caring, relatedness, and support that the Exile needed at the time of the original wounding.

The Self can provide the Exile with a new, positive experience to replace the original, painful one. The reparenting process actually lays down new neural pathways in the brain. This is why your psyche and your life can change so dramatically.

During the witnessing step, the Exile showed you a memory in which it took on pain and negative beliefs (burdens). You will focus on this memory for the reparenting step. If the Exile showed you a number of related memories, you can choose one of these to focus on.

Reparenting Process

In your imagination, join the Exile in that original childhood situation. For example, if the memory involves being ridiculed by your mother for the way you are helping her in the kitchen, imagine yourself in that kitchen with that Exile and your mother. Make sure you enter the situation **as the Self**—with all your adult knowledge and capacities, enhanced by the qualities of the Self, such as compassion, courage, and calmness. Be with the Exile in the way it needed someone to be with it at that time. It may need understanding,

caring, support, approval, protection from harm, encouragement, or love. Sense what is needed from you for healing in that situation and redress what happened.

When you understand what the Exile needs from you, provide it through your internal imagination. This may include visual images, body sensing, emotional contact, and talking to the Exile. From Self, you have the capacity to reparent the Exile—to be the good parent that it needs. This is very satisfying for the Exile and is also rewarding for you because it feels wonderful to provide comfort and safety to a part of you that desperately needs it. It also deepens the bond between you and the Exile.

Sometimes the Exile wants you to take action in that scene and do something for it or be its advocate. For example, it may want you to talk to its parents about a way it was treated or something it needed. Sometimes an Exile wants support to speak for itself. It may want you to stand next to or behind it as it communicates what it needed.

Don't try to make the Exile change in any way. You don't want it to feel pressure to change who it is or to think or feel differently about itself. These kinds of changes will result naturally from the reparenting experience and from the next step, which is unburdening.

Keep your focus on what you can do right now. At first, it might be easier to focus on what the Exile can get from you rather than from other people in the childhood situation. Confronting or changing the original situation is possible and is often quite helpful, but it is usually easier for the Exile to receive support from you.

If the Exile wants things from you in the future (over the next few weeks, for example), you may want to promise to give it what it wants. It is important to follow through on what you commit to, so do it carefully. However, be sure to see if there is anything the Exile needs from you right now.

EXERCISE   Reparenting an Exile

Now we are going to move on to reparenting the Exile. As before, you may want to continue to work with the Exile you worked with in a previous exercise, or you may want to explore a new Exile. If the latter is true, make sure to work through all the previous steps so that your Protectors know you are here with the best intentions and in your highest capacities of compassion and caring for the Exile.

Wherever you choose to start, take a few moments and ground your Self energy. Take a deep breath and then imagine bringing your breath in through the top of your head and blowing it out through your toes. Imagine letting the air be like the waves of the ocean, moving through you, calming and relaxing you. This flow of air can wash away anything that keeps you from being fully in Self.

Once you have accessed and witnessed the childhood origins of an Exile's pain, ask if it would like you to enter the childhood scene or time and help it. If the Exile is willing, imagine yourself going back in time and being there with the child of the past. Let the Exile tell you what it wants to happen and what it wants from you.

As you give the Exile what it needs, check to see if it can sense you. Then check to see how it is responding to what you are giving. Is it taking it in? Take time to feel the experience of giving (the love, support, compassion, and so on). How does it feel in your body to be present with the Exile in this way? Then take time for the Exile to bask in the good feelings that result and to feel the effects in its body.

Exile: _____

What happened in childhood: _____

_____

_____

_____

How that made the Exile feel: _____

_____

The form of reparenting you gave the Exile: _____

_____

Anything the Exile wanted you to provide it with directly: _____

_____

_____

Whether the Exile wanted you to advocate for it in a situation: _____

_____

Whether the Exile wanted you to support it in advocating for itself: _____

_____

How the Exile responded to your reparenting efforts: _____

_____

How others responded to your reparenting efforts: _____

_____

Use the journal space below to take specific notes on this process.

_____

_____

_____

_____

SAMPLE   **Reparenting an Exile**

Exile: The Good Girl

What happened in childhood: Two little girls ran past her house to avoid her because they didn't want to walk to school with her.

How that made the Exile feel: Lonely, sad, like she was different or strange

The form of reparenting you gave the Exile: Self entered the scene.

Anything the Exile wanted you to provide it with directly? Yes. She wanted Self to be her friend.

Sample continued on next page

Sample continued from previous page

Whether the Exile wanted you to advocate for it in a situation: <u>No. She said,</u>
<u>"If I had you as a friend, I wouldn't need those other girls."</u>

Whether the Exile wanted you to support it in advocating for itself:
<u>She wanted support in sticking her tongue out at the other girls and</u>
<u>saying, "See, now I HAVE a friend."</u>

How the Exile responded to your reparenting efforts: <u>She relaxed, became</u>
<u>playful, and had fun.</u>

How others responded to your reparenting efforts: <u>They became</u>
<u>unimportant.</u>

EXERCISE   Reparenting an Exile in Real Time

This exercise can be used to do follow-up work with an Exile that you have already reparented and/or retrieved. Choose an Exile that you know well and have already given reparenting to.

Name of Exile: _____

Original childhood situation: _____

_____

How you reparented the Exile: _____

_____

_____

Any promises you made to the Exile: _____

_____

_____

You can set an intention to reparent this Exile in real time over the next week.

In order to be aware of when the Exile is likely to be triggered, answer the following questions:

What kinds of situations or people tend to activate this Exile? _____

_____

_____

When are these likely to occur during the next week? _____

_____

Find a way to remind yourself to be aware of whether this part becomes activated at these times. When you notice that the Exile has been triggered, take a moment to tune into it and find out what it is feeling and what it needs. Most likely, it will need the same form of reparenting that you have already given it during your time with it. This makes it easy to do because you already know what it needs. Give the Exile the reparenting it needs in the moment.

Make notes below as necessary about your experience.

Exile: _____

Time and place of trigger: _____

Trigger situation: _____

_____

_____

Awareness triggers:

Feelings: _____

Body sensations: _____

Memories: _____

Thoughts: _____

Emotions: _____

Protectors arising: _____

_____

Other responses: _____

_____

_____

Reparenting intervention: _____

_____

_____

_____

How the Exile responded? _____

_____

_____

_____

Anything else the Exile needs from you: _____

_____

_____

_____

_____

Chapter 16

RETRIEVING AN EXILE

Exiles are living in the past, reexperiencing past trauma over and over again. An important step in the healing process is giving an Exile the option of being retrieved, or taken out of the childhood environment. This is a very powerful act on its behalf. The Exile is usually shocked that this is possible.

You may need to educate the Exile more specifically as to who you are and the fact that you live in a different time in which the threats and restrictions of the past no longer apply. Let the Exile know how old you are and what your life is like now.

It is important to check with the Exile and make sure it understands that it has been living in the past and that it is possible for you to bring it into the present, where things will be different. Ask the Exile if it would like to be taken out of the past and brought to a safe, comfortable place. The Exile will probably ask where it will go. It is often appropriate to ask the Exile to choose where it would like to go.

You have a number of general options of where you can take the Exile:

- You can take it into your home to be with you in your current life.

- If your current life does not feel completely safe, you can discuss having the Exile stay with someone it feels safe with, real or imagined.

- You can bring the Exile into your body, for example, to live in your heart.

- You can create an imaginary place for the Exile to stay where it will feel safe.

- You can support the Exile's wishes regarding where it wants to go. For example, an Exile that has been confined may want to be free to roam. In that case, you can remind the Exile that your door is always open if it wants to visit or come live with you at some point in the future.

Sometimes Exiles are hesitant to be retrieved. The following are a number of possible reasons:

- Asking about retrieval may bring up issues of mistrust. The Protectors that come up around this issue need to be worked with in the same way you would work with any other Protector concern (see Chapter 8).

- The reparenting experience may have made it safer for the Exile to exist where it is. The Exile may want to stay there for a while and feel what that is like.

- Exiles may have concerns about others that they take care of. For example, some Exiles are Protectors of younger Exiles, sometimes a sibling. Usually if they hear that they can take the other Exiles with them, they have an easier time being retrieved.

- Sometimes the dynamics of the family situation are a cause for concern. The Exile may believe that it has to take care of a parent or that the family will fall apart if it leaves. This kind of enmeshment should probably be considered a burden and should be worked with as in Chapter 17.

Temporary Retrieval

It's often appropriate to work with Exiles in stages over a period of time. The retrieval process can also happen at earlier stages of the work with an Exile. If you are getting to know an Exile in a sequence of sessions, at the end of a session you might offer to take it out of the past situation and find it a safer place to stay until you meet again.

If the Exile is not ready to do this, you might offer it some kind of support while it remains in the past. A warm blanket, a flashlight, or anything else the Exile desires can make a difference while it waits to finish the work.

EXERCISE **Retrieving an Exile**

You are now going to give the Exile the opportunity to be retrieved—that is, to come out of the past and into the present. You will probably want to work with an Exile that you are very familiar with, possibly the one from the previous exercises. As before, if you start with a new Exile, remember to begin with the Protector and go through the steps for getting to know it (Steps P1–P5; see Appendix A, pages 155–156) as well as the first steps of getting to know the Exile. You could wait to do this step after reparenting, or if you are feeling at any point that staying in the past is unsafe for the Exile, you may suggest that you can bring it out.

Wherever you start, take some time to bring in Self energy. You want to be clearly in Self so that the Exile can trust you and believe that you can and will take it out of its unpleasant situation. To get in Self, it may be helpful to tense all your muscles and then breathe a deep sigh of relief as you relax them. You can also do this by muscle group: tensing and relaxing first your legs, then your lower torso, then your chest, then your arms, then your shoulders, and finally your neck and face.

Follow this with a deep life-giving breath in which you hold the inhale for a few counts and then hold the exhale for the same number of counts.

From here, remind the Protectors that you are present with the strength and compassion of Self energy and with the best of healing intentions for the Exile.

When you are in Self and are assured that the Exile is aware of you and trusts you, offer it the possibility of being retrieved.

You might say, "Are you aware that you have been living in the past? It is possible for me to help you leave this time and place and take you somewhere where you will be safe. Are you interested in doing that?"

Fill in below your experience in retrieving the Exile.

Exile: _____

Where it is in the past: _____

_____

_____

The stages of the process you have gone through with this Exile:

____ Identifying it

____ Getting permission to work with it

____ Unblending from Concerned Parts

____ Getting to know it

____ Reparenting it

____ Unburdening it

How the Exile responded when you asked it about coming out of the past and into the present: _____

_____

Exile's concerns, if any: _____

_____

How you handled those concerns: _____

_____

Where you were comfortable taking the Exile: _____

_____

Whether the Exile was comfortable going there: _____

_____

How you brought the Exile out: _____

_____

How the Exile responded to being out of the past: _____

_____

_____

Use the journal space below to take specific notes on this process.

_____

_____

_____

_____

_____

SAMPLE **Retrieving an Exile**

Exile: The Good Girl

Where it is in the past:

Second grade, having trouble with friends at a new school

The stages of the process you have gone through with this Exile:

  __X__ Identifying it

  __X__ Getting permission to work with it

  __X__ Unblending from Concerned Parts

  __X__ Getting to know it

  __X__ Reparenting it

  _____ Unburdening it

How the Exile responded when you asked it about coming out of the past and

  into the present: She was happy to come into the present.

How you brought the Exile out: I walked into the scene, took her hand,

  and walked her into the present with me.

Where you were comfortable taking the Exile: To be with me in my current

  life, where we can play together

Whether the Exile was comfortable going there: She was delighted to come.

How the Exile responded to being out of the past: She felt free and safe.

Chapter 17

UNBURDENING AN EXILE

Once you have accessed and witnessed the childhood origins of an Exile's pain and you have reparented and retrieved the Exile, the next major step is unburdening. This is an internal ritual of healing.

As mentioned in Chapter 14, a burden is an extreme feeling, memory, energy, or belief about oneself or about the world that a part has taken on as a result of childhood trauma, a specific incident, a relationship, or another painful situation. The burden is not natural to the part and therefore can be released.

Preparing an Exile for Unburdening

Once you have clearly identified the burden or burdens associated with the situation you have been witnessing, ask the Exile, "Do you want to give up or release the burden that you have been carrying?" The part may jump at the opportunity to get rid of all that negativity, or it may be confused or reluctant (see below).

The Unburdening Process

When the Exile is ready, ask the part where it carries the burden in or on its body. The part can feel this and/or see it, preferably both. For example, it might experience the burden as black glop in its heart, agitation in the abdomen, or a yucky feeling all over.

Ask the Exile what it would like to release its burden to. The burden can be released to one of the natural elements: given up to the light, washed away by water, blown away by wind, buried in the earth, burned up in fire, or anything else that feels right. The part may instead want to give the burden up to a spiritual figure, such as God, Jesus, Mohammed, or an angel. Almost any image that allows the part to release what it has been holding is fine.

From the place of Self, help the Exile to arrange the situation so it can release the burden in whatever way it wants. Allow as much time as is needed for this process. You will probably feel the burden leaving the Exile's body as it is released. You could suggest that the part tell you when it is finished, or check with it during the process. Make sure that the part knows that it has as much time as it needs. If it can't release everything at this time, let it know it can release more at another time or as things come up. Check its body to see if anything else that doesn't belong to it needs to be released.

Positive Qualities

Once the burden is released, the Exile is free to become more of what it truly is at its core. Notice what positive qualities or feelings arise in the part once the burden is gone. Unburdened parts often feel joy, strength, playfulness, freedom, love, or other similar qualities. A good question to ask the part is, "What qualities that would be helpful in the future do you want to take in?" As each quality comes up, let the part take time to breathe it in separately. Allow some time for the part to feel the infusion of the specific quality, and suggest that it let itself fully enjoy these experiences. As it does, feel how they manifest in your body.

What Does the Part Want to Do Now?

Younger parts often want to just go out and play or be in a place where they can be free. Some parts want to stay in certain parts of your body, such as your heart, your head, or your belly. Some parts need to rest for a while and make up their minds later. Anything that feels like a step toward healing is fine.

Reluctance to Unburden

Here are some of the commonest reasons that Exiles may resist unburdening:

- The Exile may be confused about the idea of unburdening and not understand what the term means.

Response: You can explain further that the memories, feelings, pain, beliefs, and confusions that the Exile holds are from the past. They are not who the part is—just what it holds. It is possible to release those things and let them go.

- The part may have some concerns about who it will be without the burdens to identify it.
  Response: You can assure the Exile that you will help it handle that situation when the time comes. The part will have some choice about who it is.

- The Exile may be reluctant or frightened to let go of the burdens.
  Response: Ask it, "Why are you attached to this burden?" or "What are you afraid would happen if you let this burden go?" You can help the Exile handle its fears.

- Sometimes when an Exile doesn't feel ready to unburden, something else needs to happen first—more witnessing, more trust of Self, fuller reparenting or retrieval, and so on. There also might be another part that doesn't want the burden to be released.
  Response: Work with the Exile to identify what is needed and address the issues one by one until they are all taken care of. Don't proceed with the unburdening until the part is completely ready.

- Sometimes the part may only be ready to release some of the burden.
  Response: You can give the Exile permission to let go of a percentage of the burden but not all of it. You can then unburden that percentage and come back to the issue in a future session.

Unburdening is just the final step in a long path toward healing. All the preceding steps are just as important.

EXERCISE   Unburdening an Exile

We are now going to unburden an Exile. You will want to work with an Exile that you know well—either one from a previous exercise or one that you have moved through all of the previous steps. This is usually done after the Exile has been retrieved, but that is not necessary. You can still unburden an Exile if something has shifted in the original situation and the Exile has decided to stay.

Before you make contact with the Exile, reaffirm that you are in Self and that the Protectors recognize that you are.

You might take a few deep breaths and surround yourself with a colored or white light. You might bring this light in through the crown of your head and let it fill your body, bringing you peace, clarity, compassion, or any other Self quality.

Take a deep breath, confirm that you still have permission from any Protector that has been involved, and make contact with the Exile.

Present the idea of unburdening to the Exile. You might say, "I can help you get rid of the burdens that you have been carrying. You can release all those bad feelings, memories, negative thoughts, pain, and confusions from the past. Do you want to do that?"

Help the Exile through any reluctance it might have.

Fill in below your experience of unburdening the Exile.

Exile: _____

What happened in childhood: _____

_____

_____

_____

How that made the Exile feel: _____

_____

_____

_____

The form of reparenting you gave the Exile: _____

_____

_____

If the Exile was retrieved, where you took it: _____

_____

Burdens the Exile carries: _____

_____

_____

Concerns the Exile has about unburdening: _____

_____

_____

Ways you handled its concerns: _____

_____

_____

Where the Exile carries the burdens in its body: _____

_____

The element, spiritual figure, or other place or thing the burdens were released to:

_____

Positive qualities that emerged: _____

_____

_____

Where the part wanted to stay: _____

_____

_____

Use the journal space below to take specific notes on this process.

_____

_____

_____

_____

SAMPLE **Unburdening an Exile**

Exile: The Good Girl

What happened in childhood: Rejected by friends at a new school

How that made the Exile feel: Lonely, rejected, and as if there was something wrong with her

The form of reparenting you gave the Exile: Self came in to be her friend.

If the Exile was retrieved, where you took it: Yes, taken home with me

Burdens the Exile carries: Feeling weird and unacceptable. Rejected by friends and not supported by new teachers at school. She feels devalued and not accepted for who she is.

Concerns the Exile has about unburdening: Wants to make sure that I will be her friend

Ways you handled its concerns: I assured her that I would be her friend.

Where the Exile carries the burdens in its body: Shoulders; she has hunched posture, collapsed chest to protect pain in heart, and ungrounded feet.

What element, spiritual figure, or other place or thing the burdens were released to: Went into the forest and dug a big hole to put the burden in, and poured water from the creek over her to cleanse her. Then she danced around the hole like an Indian.

Positive qualities that emerged: Playfulness, spontaneity, curiosity

Where the part wanted to stay: Home with me

Chapter 18

INTEGRATION &
UNBURDENING PROTECTORS

Once you have unburdened an Exile, it is important to integrate this work with the rest of your internal system, especially those Protectors that have been protecting against this Exile's feelings. They may or may not already be aware of the work that has been done.

Checking with Protectors

Check with each Protector to see if it has been aware of the work you have done with the Exile. You may want to introduce one or more Protectors to the transformed Exile.

If a Protector is no longer easily accessible, ask it to come forward. See how the Protector feels about the work that has been done. Check to see if the Protector now realizes that its protective role is no longer necessary.

Protector Concerns About Giving Up Its Role

- The Protector may still be protecting other Exiles and may therefore still need to maintain its role in some way.

  Response: In this case, you must unburden the other Exiles before the Protector will completely let go of its role. You can check to see if there are some changes it can make because of the shift with the current Exile. If so, assist it in clarifying those changes.

- The Protector may not be ready to let go of its role.

  Response: Ask the Protector, "What are you afraid would happen if you gave up your role or stopped doing your job?" This may uncover other Exiles or Protectors it is polarized with or other fears it has. You can work with these parts from Self.

- The Protector may be afraid that the change won't last.

  Response: Let it know that you (Self) will be there to take care of that, if necessary.

Unburdening Protectors

Protectors have burdens, too, though they are not the same as an Exile's. An Exile's burden is pain, whereas a Protector's burden is its protective role. That role is not natural to the Protector—it was taken on because the Protector perceived a great danger to you. Once that danger is no longer there, the burden of this protective role can be released.

Sometimes this realization causes a spontaneous unburdening in the Protector. It feels free to take on a new role and can easily identify who it wants to become.

Sometimes a Protector wants to go through an unburdening process. In this case, the burden is the protective role itself. The Protector took on its extreme role at a specific time in your life. It holds this history in the form of memories, beliefs, confusions, and identifications. To release the Protector from its role, you can help it go through the same process used to unburden an Exile (see Chapter 17).

In some cases, it may be necessary to access the childhood memories from the time when the Protector took on its extreme role. These may or may not be the same as those of the Exile. The Protector's childhood memories need to be witnessed by Self before the burden can be released.

New Qualities

As with the Exile, after the Protector's burden is released, positive qualities may spontaneously arise. It might be a feeling of "I want to feel capable, strong, free, compassionate," and so on. You can ask the Protector, "What qualities would you like to take in that would be helpful to you in the future?" Give the Protector time to take in one quality at a time, moving gently with the breath while allowing each quality be assimilated.

New Role

Whether or not the Protector does an unburdening ritual, let it know that it can choose a new role in your psyche. This is especially important for a Protector. Its role may be a non-extreme version of the role it had, the opposite of its previous role, or something entirely different. It may want to establish a new relationship with the Exile. If its new role involves any other parts, check with them to see how they feel about the change.

Check with Other Parts

Once the work with the Protector and Exile is complete, ask if there are any parts that have feelings or concerns about the work you have done and the changes that have happened. For example, if the work brought love, spontaneity, or strength into the system, there may be parts that are threatened by that. You can reassure them about their fears or plan to work with them next.

Sometimes Doubting Parts come up that do not trust the work that was done or are afraid it won't last. These parts need to be heard and accepted. They may need something from you or from one of the other parts, or they may be invited to watch what happens over time.

Testing

After all this work, it is a good idea to test the results against the original trailhead that activated the Protector. For example, if the original Protector was a part that tried to please authority figures, it would be useful to imagine yourself in a situation with an authority figure in your current life and then notice what parts (if any) get activated. This will give you an idea of whether the Exile and Protector have been truly unburdened and whether any other parts may also be reacting to this situation. Testing prepares you for facing the real-life situation and lets you know what further work you may need to do.

Follow-Up

It's a good idea to check in periodically with the parts that have been unburdened, especially Exiles, to see how they are. As you complete the work with a part, it may want to be sure that you will follow up with it. It may want regular contact or may want to be allowed play time. You might ask the part what it would like and then plan how to make good on your promises.

EXERCISE   **Releasing a Protector**

We are now going to work with the Protector that has been connected to an unburdened Exile. Begin this process at the point at which you can go back and focus on a Protector whose Exile has been unburdened.

Take a moment to activate Self energy. You might try sitting up straight, putting your hand over your heart, taking a deep breath, and chanting a sound. OM is a good sound that vibrates the heart. Hmmmm or various vowel sounds have been found to vibrate different energy centers. You can experiment and see what brings you into your center today.

When you feel present in Self, focus your attention on the Protector. What is your sense of it in this moment? Has it changed much since you started working with it? Make sure that it knows who you are. You can ask it, "Have you been watching what has been happening with the Exile that you were protecting? Does it seem as though your role has changed? Would you also like to be unburdened?"

Fill in below your experience of releasing a Protector.

Protector: _____

Protector's role: _____

Exile's burden: _____

Is the Protector now ready to let go of its role? _____

If not, why not?

_____ It's protecting other Exiles.

_____ It's afraid to let go of its role.

_____ It's afraid the change won't last.

_____ Another concern _____

How do you help the Protector with its concerns so that it feels more comfortable

with the unburdening process? _____

When you unburden the Protector, what does it want to release its burden to?

_____

What qualities that the Protector wanted to take in would be most helpful in the

future? _____

_____

What new role, if any, would it like to play? _____

Are there any parts that are uncomfortable with these changes? _____

_____

What are their concerns? _____

_____

How did you reassure them? _____

_____

When you go back to the original situation and imagine yourself there again, what

do you feel? _____

_____

Were any parts triggered? _____

_____

Does any future work need to be done? _____

_____

_____

_____

SAMPLE   **Releasing a Protector**

Protector 1: Angry Defender

Protector's role: Keep the little girl from being hurt and rejected again by pushing people away

Exile's burden: Rejection by childhood friends and a teacher

Is the Protector now ready to let go of its role? Yes. Wants to go and play with the little girl and Self. Does not feel the need to unburden.

Protector 2: Inner Critic

Protector's role: Keep the little girl safe by criticizing her so she wouldn't take any chances with people

Is the Protector now ready to let go of its role? No.

If not, why not? It's afraid to let go of its role. Doesn't know what it would do if it didn't criticize her to protect her.

How do you help the Protector with its concerns so that it feels more comfortable with the unburdening process? I told her that she could take on a new role when she let go of the old one.

When you unburden the Protector, what does it want to release its burden to? Fire

What qualities that the Protector would like to take in would be most helpful in the future? Generosity, being carefree, peacefulness

What new role, if any, would it like to play? Support the little girl to become her best self

Are there any parts that are uncomfortable with these changes? No.

When you go back to the original situation and imagine yourself there again, what do you feel? I imagine going through the school experience with a best friend, and I see what a difference it would have made in my ability to maintain satisfying adult relationships.

EXERCISE   **Follow-Up with a Protector**

Choose a Protector that has released its protective role. You will be checking in with it during the week, whenever it could be triggered.

Preparation: To help yourself be aware at those times, answer the following questions:

What kinds of situations or people tend to activate this Protector?

_____

_____

_____

When are these likely to occur during the next week? _____

_____

What body sensations, thoughts, behavior, or emotions will let you know this Protector is triggered? _____

_____

Homework Practice

In those situations in which the Protector is usually triggered, notice whether or not it becomes activated. If it doesn't become activated, notice how you feel and act that is different from before.

Date	Situation	Thoughts	Bodily Experience	Feelings	Behavior

Appreciate the changes you have made. How do you want to celebrate your success? _____

_____

_____

If the Protector does become activated, check in to see what triggered it and what it is afraid of. _____

_____

_____

_____

_____

Keep track of this so you know what additional work is needed in a future session to complete the transformation of this Protector.

Chapter 19

ENDING A SESSION

Whenever you are ending a session, it's a good idea to respectfully connect with all the parts you have worked with thus far.

1. Thank the Target Part for making itself known to you. If you are in the process of working with it, let it know that you will come back to it. Reaffirm any agreements you have made with it during your work. If you have completed your work with it, check in and see how it's doing.

2. If you've worked with a Protector and it has given you permission to work with an Exile, thank the Protector and see how it feels about the work you've done with the Exile.

3. Thank any Concerned Parts for stepping aside to allow you to do the work. Check with them about whether they've seen the work that you did and how it has affected them.

See if any other parts need to say anything before you stop. Acknowledge them and spend some time addressing their concerns.

Chapter 20

WORKING WITH A PARTNER

The Importance of Partner Work

To get the most out of this workbook, you need to practice IFS on a regular basis. Each chapter outlines a basic idea with exercises that bring home the concepts, making them relevant to your psyche and your life. For most people, it works best to do these with a partner; the two of you take turns working on yourselves with the other as witness and facilitator. It isn't easy to open up deep places of pain in yourself, even with the powerful and respectful IFS method. When someone is there to witness you, it makes the whole exploration more inviting by providing a holding environment for your wounded and defended parts. Even a silent witness provides presence and support that is very helpful for most people.

What Partner Work Could Look Like

Before you begin your explorations, have a discussion with your partner about the kind of facilitation you would like when you're working. If you're new to this process, we recommend that, at the beginning of your work together, you act as a quiet witness. Gradually, as you become more comfortable with the IFS process, and perhaps also with the partner relationship, you can move to more active witnessing and finally to gentle facilitation.

The Explorer

When you are the explorer, you are in charge of the session and are responsible for what happens. This is different from being in psychotherapy, where the therapist has more responsibility for the work. When you are working with a friend in peer counseling, he or she can be helpful to you but may not know any more about IFS and therapy than you do. Therefore, he or she can't take responsibility for what happens in the session the way a therapist would. It is up to you to conduct the session in a way that works for you. It is your job to judge how fast or slow to take the process and how deeply to explore certain issues. **You** are in charge of keeping track of what's happening in the session and where you are in the IFS procedure. You are responsible for choosing what parts of yourself to explore and how far to go into painful or vulnerable places in your psyche. Although the listener has an important role to play, it is your show.

Listener Possibilities

Stage 1: Quiet Witness

Your job is to stay in Self as much as possible. Before you begin, take some time to center and ground. Feel yourself supported by the chair you're in, follow your breath for a while, and ask any parts that are active to give you some space to be present.

While your partner is exploring, do not speak unless he or she asks for your help. This helps cement the idea that the explorer is in charge and responsible for the session. It helps the explorer learn how to work on him- or herself, and it encourages you to be free of any sense of responsibility for what happens. You will have an opportunity to give the explorer feedback after each session.

As your partner is exploring, you can note, for yourself, what parts come up for you. Gently acknowledge each part and ask it to give you some space to be fully present with your partner.

Stage 2: Active Witnessing

When you are an active witness, you may offer gentle suggestions at appropriate moments, during a pause, or when it seems as if your partner is at an impasse. It is up to the explorer to decide whether or not to take your suggestions. Remember that if your partner gets stuck or lost, it is his or her job to figure out how to proceed. This is part of the explorer's process. He or she might be confused for a while and have to work it through. You can help in any way that seems right, but you aren't obligated to "fix" the explorer, remove any pain, or get him or her out of a corner. The active witness checks to see if a suggestion at this time might be helpful, makes observations, or—with permission—expresses curiosity about something that is going on in the work. Don't find solutions or give advice. Support the process and trust its unfolding.

Stage 3: Facilitation

When both you and your partner feel ready, discuss the possibility of you more actively facilitating his or her exploration. Take this individually and move at your own pace. One of you might be ready for this before the other. Moving into this slowly gives you the leeway to become comfortable with the process before you take an active role. You will gradually learn to be helpful without having the burden of knowing what to say thrust on you too soon. Remember that your presence and full attention are very helpful to the explorer's process, even if you don't say a word.

Facilitation Possibilities

Here are some possibilities for facilitating your partner to explore him- or herself. It can be useful to follow along with the Help Sheets (see Appendix A) and keep track of which step the explorer is on. Taking notes on the parts that have come up and been related to can often be helpful.

- Reflect back what the person (or a part) is feeling.

- Mention when you think a Concerned Part is getting in the way and the explorer doesn't realize it.

- Mention when you think the person is blended with the Target Part and doesn't realize it.

- Suggest questions to ask a part. Some effective phrasing is, "You might ask the part…" This leaves the person room to not take your suggestion.

- Suggest which step the person might do next. This can be in the form of a question to ask the part, as in the previous item. Or it could be done by mentioning the step explicitly, for example, "Maybe it is time for Reparenting now."

- Point out when you think a part is an Exile or Protector when that may influence what happens next. For example, "Shouldn't you get to know that Protector better before working with the Exile?"

- Point out when it looks as though the person has switched to a new part without realizing it.

- Keep track of the original Target Part when the explorer is working with some Concerned Parts so you can help your partner refocus when appropriate.

- Keep track of Concerned Parts and Protectors that have stepped aside so they can be checked in with and thanked at the end of the session.

Remember that the person working is in charge of the session. You don't have to do the above facilitations. Only say something when it feels to you as if it will be helpful.

Explorer: Remember that you are in charge of the session. Don't feel that you have to take your partner's suggestions.

Feedback

When working with a partner, after the explorer has finished working, it can be helpful for the partner to offer feedback about the work. Don't give feedback only on the content of what the explorer worked on. Focus especially on the IFS process.

People can feel quite vulnerable when they have been doing this kind of exploration, so it is important to give feedback that is sensitive and supportive. Before you and your partner begin working together, it is important to have a conversation about feedback preferences. Each of you has a right to ask for, or to limit, feedback. The type of feedback does not have to be the same for both of you.

Here are some possibilities:

- You can talk about any personal responses you had to the explorer's work as long as the responses aren't negative or likely to be hurtful. It is best to do this by talking about parts of you that you noticed were activated.

- You can say how moved you were by the work or any other positives responses.

- You can mention ways that you have similar issues to what the explorer was working on. Be considerate when sharing your issues. You want to keep the focus on the explorer as long as he or she needs to process the experience. When it is time to shift the focus, you can have your fuller experience.

- You can ask the explorer questions that might further his or her understanding of the work. You might note where his or her work piqued your curiosity.

- You can mention any steps of the IFS process that he or she skipped over.

- You can mention any parts that you thought were blended with Self.

- You can mention any parts that you thought were activated that the explorer didn't seem to notice.

Make sure that your feedback is not given in a judgmental way.

If the explorer feels judged by any of the feedback, it is good to say so in order to prevent this from happening in the future. Give the explorer some time to explore whether he or she had parts come up that were reacting to your feedback.

This is not a time to give advice. Your role as listener is to be supportive of the explorer's process and trust that working with parts in an honest way will lead to the clarity he or she needs to live more fully.

Ongoing Partner Relationships

Before you start each session, create an understanding between you about how much facilitation and what type the explorer wants. Do you want to be led through each step and have questions suggested? Do you want to primarily lead yourself and have your partner intervene only when help is needed? This can change from session to session, so check in each time. It is also important to revisit this during the session if it needs to be renegotiated or if something isn't working.

If you work with someone regularly, pay attention to anything going on between you that may be getting in the way of your work. Bring it up with your partner and work it through by talking about the feelings that your parts have. The partner relationship can be a fruitful exploration. Make sure to bring any issue out into the open first and let your partner know that you're interested in investigating your parts around it.

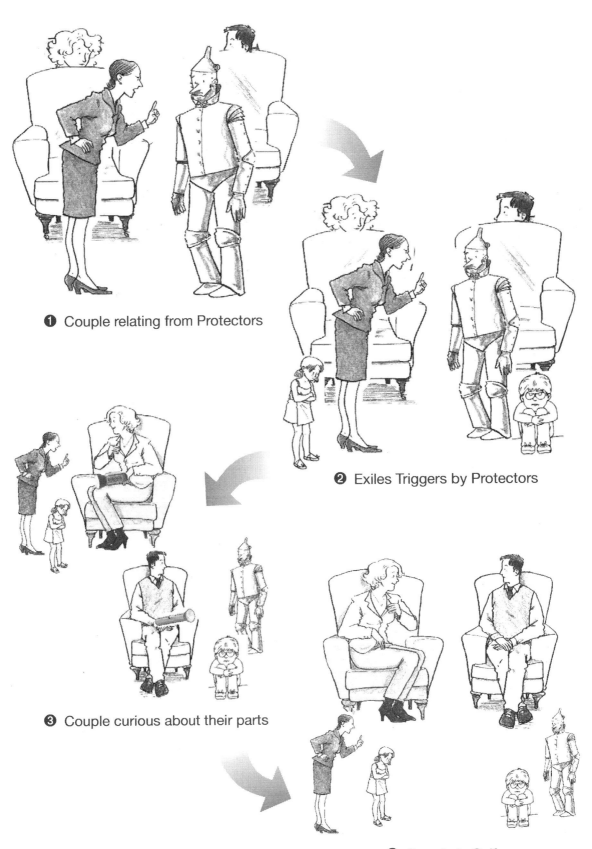

❶ Couple relating from Protectors

❷ Exiles Triggers by Protectors

❸ Couple curious about their parts

❹ Couple in Self

Chapter 21

IFS WITH COUPLES

with Marla Silverman, PhD

We are now going to take what you've learned about your own internal system and see how it plays out in couple's relationships.

All people want to feel heard and met. You do and your partner does. This is true at the deepest level under all the fears.

The hope we bring when we enter into a relationship is that we will finally have someone who cares for us, protects us, and has our best interests at heart. We hope that our longings will be met, our young inner children will be nurtured, and our Exiles will be healed.

Let's look at what happens to those needs, hopes, and longings as they encounter the needs, hopes, and longings of your partner. What happens when you feel hurt, angry, disappointed, or even wounded? What happens when your partner experiences your Protectors as insensitive or vice versa?

Difficulties in Partner Interactions

When we get stuck, it often looks like this:

1. We interpret our partner's behavior as hurtful—insensitive and uncaring.

2. We feel hurt and perhaps angry.

3. Our Protectors rise up—for example, we pursue, withdraw, explain, demand, blame, or shame.

4. Our partner feels attacked, unseen, unmet, misunderstood, and abandoned.

5. Our partner's Protectors rise up to diminish his or her hurt.

6. We feel frustrated, unhappy, and perhaps hopeless that we can ever get through to our partner.

When we are able to come from Self, our creative capacities and our ability to consider both our partner and ourself are available. Instead of reliving old patterns of beliefs and reactivity, we can:

- listen internally and hear our activated parts—our Protectors and the hurt Exiles they protect

- bring appreciation to our Protectors for their loyalty and devotion

- send compassion to our Exiles

- protect our Exiles from a Self-led place

- speak **for** these parts, letting our partner know what we are experiencing internally

When we move out of reactivity, with its demands and blame, our partner can begin to experience us as safer. When others feel safe with us, they are more able to come from Self rather than from their reactive parts. These are the moments of genuine Self-to-Self contact. When we are in that state with each other, we create mutual understanding, respect, compassion, friendship, and openheartedness.

Couples frequently find themselves having the same fight over and over again. They often are unaware of their feelings or the parts that are activated. The same parts of one partner trigger familiar parts of another. It can be helpful to track these dialogues and look further into them to see what feelings are being experienced and what parts are showing up.

SAMPLE **Couples Sample #1: Repetitive Dialogue**

Here is an example of one couple's repetitive dialogue:

Chris said:
I had a really difficult day at work again today.

Terry said:
Yeah, I did, too.

Chris said:
You never ask me about my work. You know I'm having trouble.

Terry said:
You talk about your work all the time. You were complaining about your boss all last night.

Chris said:
Yeah, I talked, but you weren't really listening.

Terry said:
I listened for half an hour.

Chris said:
Could have fooled me. You didn't seem the least bit interested.

Terry said:
There's nothing I can ever do to please you. It's never enough.

Chris said:
You're so callous, you only care about yourself.

Terry said:
You're impossible. I can't talk to you.

Chris said:
You always pull out when the going gets rough.

EXERCISE   **Tracking Repetitive Interactions**

Think about your interactions with your partner. We often find ourselves falling into repetitive dialogues that leave us feeling frustrated and unheard. Use the space below to write out one such dialogue.

I said:

She/He said:

I said:

She/He said:

I said:

She/He said:

I said:

She/He said:

I said:

She/He said:

I said:

SAMPLE   **Couples Sample #2: Feelings During Dialogue**

Here we can look at the feelings that Chris and Terry were experiencing during their dialogue:

Chris said: I had a really difficult day at work again today.	*Chris felt:* Vulnerable and inadequate at work and afraid of being exposed. Needy of reassurance.

	Terry said: Yeah, I did, too.	*Terry felt:* Disregarded, like my needs and problems don't matter. Thought: When is it about me? Chris is always complaining about work, and I have my own problems.

Chris said: You never ask me about my work. You know I'm having trouble.	*Chris felt:* Alone and uncared about.

	Terry said: You talk about your work all the time. You were complaining about it all last night.	*Terry felt:* Hurt that Chris doesn't recognize how I tried to be supportive last night.

Chris said: Yeah, I talked, but you weren't really listening.	*Chris felt:* Hurt that Terry wasn't providing the support I need.

	Terry said: I listened for half an hour.	*Terry felt:* Defensive, unappreciated, and unrecognized.

Chris said:	Chris felt:	
Could have fooled me. You didn't seem the least bit interested.	Angry and defensive.	

	Terry said:	Terry felt:
	There's nothing I can ever do to please you. It's never enough.	Judgmental of Chris and inadequate and unable to make Chris happy.

Chris said:	Chris felt:	
You're so callous, you only care about yourself.	Judged and protective.	

	Terry said:	Terry felt:
	You're impossible. I can't talk to you.	Inadequate, alone, and hopeless.

Chris said:	Chris felt:	
You always pull out when the going gets rough.	Abandoned.	

EXERCISE Tracking Feelings During Dialogue

Use the worksheet on pages 138–139 to fill in the feelings that arose during your repetitive dialogue. Take a moment to reflect on what you were feeling during the dialogue. If you're working with your partner, you might want to fill it in together. If you're working alone, spend some time feeling into your partner's side of the interaction. See if you can come from a compassionate Self. How well do you know your own feelings? What do you understand about your partner's feelings, triggers, and parts? What underlies both of your reactions?

SAMPLE **Couples Sample #3:**
Parts Holding Feelings in the Dialogue

Our parts hold our feelings. Here are the parts that were probably triggered during Chris and Terry's dialogue. As we have learned, all parts have positive intentions for us. Here we explore the probable intentions of the triggered parts:

Chris said:	*Chris felt:*	*What the part wanted:*
I had a really difficult day at work again today.	Vulnerable and inadequate at work and afraid of being exposed. Needy of reassurance. ***Activated Part:*** Insecure Part	To get some caring and reassurance that Chris is okay.

Terry said:	*Terry felt:*	*What the part wanted:*
Yeah, I did, too.	When is it about me? Chris is always complaining about work, and I have my own problems. ***Activated Part:*** Invisible Part that feels as though I can't ask for what I want	To signal that I have problems, too. Protection from empty feeling of having my needs dismissed.

Chris said:	*Chris felt:*	*What the part wanted:*
You never ask me about my work. You know I'm having trouble.	Alone and uncared about. ***Activated Part:*** Abandoned Child	To be heard and cared for.

Terry said:	*Terry felt:*	*What the part wanted:*
You talk about your work all the time. You were complaining about your boss all last night.	Alone and uncared about. ***Activated Part:*** Unrecognized Child	To get some recognition and acknowledgment for efforts made.

Chris said:	*Chris felt:*	*What the part wanted:*
Yeah, I talked, but you weren't really listening.	Hurt that Terry wasn't providing the support I needed. **Activated Part:** Hurt Child	To have hurt feelings recognized.

Terry said:	*Terry felt:*	*What the part wanted:*
I listened for half an hour.	Defensive, not appreciated or recognized. **Activated Part:** Protective Part	Recognition.

Chris said:	*Chris felt:*	*What the part wanted:*
Could have fooled me. You didn't seem the least bit interested.	Angry and defensive. **Activated Part:** Angry Protector	Protection from feelings of hurt and unimportance.

Terry said:	*Terry felt:*	*What the part wanted:*
There's nothing I can ever do to please you. It's never enough.	Judgmental of Chris and inadequate and unable to make Chris happy. **Activated Part:** Angry Protector	To not feel inadequate.

Chris said:	*Chris felt:*	*What the part wanted:*
You're so callous, you only care about yourself.	Judged and protective. **Activated Part:** Angry Protector	To create a wall of safety for hurt parts.

Terry said:	*Terry felt:*	*What the part wanted:*
You're impossible. I can't talk to you.	Inadequate, alone, helpless. **Activated Part:** Angry Protector	To protect inadequate, alone, and hopeless parts.

Chris said:	*Chris felt:*	*What the part wanted:*
You always pull out when the going gets rough.	Angry, abandoned. **Activated Part:** Angry Protector	To protect Abandoned Child.

EXERCISE **Tracking the Parts That Hold Feelings**

As described on page 135, first use the worksheet below to fill in the feelings that arose during your repetitive dialogue (see sample on pages 134–135).

Next, explore the parts that were triggered in the dialogue. What was the positive intention of each of your parts? Ask each part what it wanted for you. Repeating the question "What would I have if I got that?" will help you go through layers of the process and get closer to the core of each part's positive intention.

Then, as before, see if you can feel into your partner's experience and imagine what his or her parts deeply wanted for him or her.

I said:	*I felt:* **Activated Part:**	*What the part wanted for me:*

She/He said:	*She/He felt:* **Activated Part:**	*What the part wanted for her/him:*

I said:	*I felt:* **Activated Part:**	*What the part wanted for me:*

She/He said:	*She/He felt:* **Activated Part:**	*What the part wanted for her/him:*

I said:	I felt: **Activated Part:**	What the part wanted for me:

She/He said:	She/He felt: **Activated Part:**	What the part wanted for her/him:

I said:	I felt: **Activated Part:**	What the part wanted for me:

She/He said:	She/He felt: **Activated Part:**	What the part wanted for her/him:

I said:	I felt: **Activated Part:**	What the part wanted for me:

She/He said:	She/He felt: **Activated Part:**	What the part wanted for her/him:

I said:	I felt: **Activated Part:**	What the part wanted for me:

Now that you have explored your reactive behavior and the parts that were triggered for you, and have spent time feeling into and imagining your partner's behavior and triggered parts, experience what it is like to step back and see the bigger picture:

- the safety you are each trying to achieve
- how you each hurt one another when you are trying to protect yourself
- how you each see the other as an obstacle to your safety and happiness when you are reactive
- that each of you wants to feel seen, heard, understood, and cared for
- that your vulnerable Exile Parts need to be nurtured from your Self

From this bigger, grounded experience of Self, you can have compassion for yourself, your partner, and what it is like being human.

When you can do this, you are able to thoughtfully choose the moment to approach your partner and talk about the difficulties you get into together.

Remember to take it slow and to stop if either of you gets activated and can't get back to a calmer, Self-led place.

You have probably experienced the difficult interaction you are working on for some time. So going gradually, a little at a time, with patience and respect will bring you to the goal of healthy relating faster and more surely than rushing it.

This is the work that builds the trust you are both longing for.

We do not all grow at the same pace. If your partner is not yet ready to work on him- or herself, do not push. By seeing where he or she is stuck and being able to nurture your own hurt and wounded parts, you will not get into the same painful dynamic. It takes two people in a relationship to create a dynamic but only one to change it. When you can see and accept (not necessarily like) that your partner can't give you what you want in this moment, you can back off and perhaps try again another time.

We wish you patience and compassion as you grow and develop trust in yourself and your partner.

Chapter 22
WORKING WITH POLARIZED PARTS[1]

Two parts are polarized when they are in conflict with each other and each part feels that it needs to be extreme in order to counter the other part's extreme feelings or actions. The two parts are often polarized about a specific action or decision that they disagree about. This is more than just having two parts that are the opposite or even two parts that are in conflict with each other. When parts are polarized, each part is acting the way it is in order to compensate for what the other part is doing or what it believes the other part will do. Even if two parts are opposites, they aren't polarized unless each part is fighting with the other over an action, decision, or feeling. If one part is not engaged in the battle, it isn't polarization. There can be more than one part on each side of a polarization, such as polarized teams of allied parts.

When working with polarizations, you must be interested in and get to know the part(s) on each side. A Protector Part often can't release its extreme role until the part it is polarized with has also released its role, and if both feel that way, you must work with the two of them at the same time to make this possible. Dick Schwartz uses the example of a sailboat with each opposing part being a sailor that is leaning out over his side of the boat. Each fears that if he lets up even a little bit, the boat will capsize in the other's direction. The Self must work with the parts to help them ease in together.

When two parts are polarized, one part can take over for a while, and the other part can give up. This can happen for a few hours or days or years. Sometimes they then switch, and the other part takes over.

Even though both polarized parts are being extreme, most of them hold an energy or quality that is important to you. You just need to have it in a non-extreme

---

1. For a more detailed discussion of this process, see *Resolving Inner Conflict* by Jay Earley.

form. Therefore, you don't want to erase or diminish the positive energy of each part. You aren't looking to find a bland compromise between the parts or a negotiated settlement that is purely intellectual. The goal is to have the parts appreciate each other's strengths and good intentions and learn to cooperate. This leads to a much greater availability of creativity and power, and very often to innovative solutions to conflicts that are completely satisfying for both parts.

Typically polarized parts:

Food Controller vs. Indulger

Taskmaster vs. Procrastinator

Anger vs. Good Boy/Girl

Dependent Part or Merged Part vs. Distancer

Name two parts you have that are polarized:

Part A _____   Part B _____

Parts that aren't polarized:

Swimmer — Reader

Artist — Mother

Worker — Sportsperson

Name two parts you have that are *not* polarized:

Part A _____   Part B _____

Managers and Firefighters

To understand polarization more clearly, it is necessary to recognize that there are two kinds of Protectors: Managers and Firefighters. Managers are the more strategic, organized, rational parts. They are the parts of us that operate in everyday life to keep us functioning. Their roles range from keeping a semblance of order and regularity in our lives to being the backbone of our capacity to achieve and excel. Managers try to arrange our lives and our psyches so that the pain of Exiles never arises. Examples of Managers are:

The Achiever, The Judge, the Inner Critic, the Parent, the Son or Daughter, the Housekeeper, the Good Boy/Girl, and the Friend.

Firefighters are more like an emergency operating system. They are impulsive, spontaneous, nonrational, reactive, and often rash. They react to a situation with-out seriously considering the consequences of their actions. Firefighters get triggered by the threat of the feelings of the Exiles they protect breaking through to the surface. Firefighters respond impulsively just after an Exile is triggered to try to distract you from the pain or banish it from consciousness. You may not be aware of the pain starting to arise—only the Fire-fighter's reaction.

Managers are preemptive, and Firefighters are reactive. If Managers are the adults and Exiles the children, Firefighters are the teenagers, reacting impulsively to put out the fire of the Exile's pain.

Typical Firefighters are parts that act out addictions to drugs, alcohol, rage, thrill seeking, sex, eating, shopping, gambling, reading, TV, and so on. Firefighters can also take the form of a number of numbing or fogging parts such as headaches, distraction, dissociation, or falling asleep.

Firefighters are sometimes less verbal and harder to negotiate with than Managers. You may have to spend more time just being with a Firefighter in order to gain its trust. If it is resistant, don't push to get it to respond to you or tell you about itself. Just hang out with it, and over time it will slowly begin to trust you enough to reveal itself to you.

It can be much harder to be in Self with respect to Firefighters because they are often so destructive and are also hard to communicate with. This makes it hard to appreciate their attempts to protect you. Remember that they are doing what they think is necessary to protect you from intolerable pain.

Managers respond to reason. You are usually able to talk with them about their situation and their strategies for protecting their Exiles, and you're likely to be able to negotiate a plan for help and healing. In contrast, Firefighters respond to hope. Once you understand why a Firefighter does its role, it is helpful to ask a question about a possible new role for the part: "If we could heal that Exile so you didn't have to do this role, what would you prefer to do?" This may give the Firefighter hope that it can let go of the role it feels stuck in. At that point, it will grant you permission to work with the Exile.

Types of Polarizations

Firefighters and Managers are often polarized with each other. Since Firefighter activity is often dangerous and self-destructive, Managers are often judgmental of Firefighters and try to stop them or limit their behavior. Firefighters tend to be oriented toward excitement and intensity, and Managers toward control and order. You may have to work with this polarization before you can get permission to contact the Exiles that these parts are protecting. Polarizations can also exist between two Managers, two Firefighters, or either a Manager or Firefighter with an Exile.

Typical Places to Recognize Polarization

- **Trailhead:** When you explore a trailhead, you may often realize that you have opposite or conflicting responses to the situation.

  Example: You have a fight with a friend and are exploring parts at the trailhead of your reaction. One part is angry and wants to act out in a way that will make the friend jealous. Another part is afraid of being seen as bad and being judged for that behavior. That part wants to act in a conciliatory manner. These parts seem locked in combat over how you should respond.

- **Protector Fears:** When you ask a Protector what it is afraid would happen if it didn't do its role, sometimes it is afraid of the actions of a polarized part (rather than the Exile it is protecting).

  Example: You are considering making an investment. You have a Protector that keeps cautioning you about the possible loss of principal. When asked about its role, it says it is afraid you would be fooled into trusting the wrong people. When you explore it further, you find that you have a Pleaser Part that is afraid to challenge others and ask confrontational questions. The parts seem to be working against each other.

- **Resistant Concerned Part:** When you are attempting to get to know a part and a Concerned Part is interfering with your being in Self, the Concerned Part may be polarized with the Target Part.

  Example: You're trying to work on a project, and you keep doing other things. You become curious about your Procrastinator Part and start to explore it. You have a Concerned Part that is very judgmental, calling it lazy and not being willing to step aside and give you a chance to get to know the Procrastinator. This may be a Taskmaster Part that is frequently polarized with the Procrastinator.

- **Manager vs. Firefighter Polarization:** Because Firefighters' actions can be destructive, Managers will try to stop or limit them.

  Example: A Firefighter that is triggered by a stressful situation—say a job loss— might want to run away or go on a bender. An Inner Controller will try to stop or limit the Firefighter or be very shaming and critical if the Firefighter does act out.

- **Internal Battle:** If you think you are in Self and are battling with a part that you think is being destructive, this may actually be a polarization. Self doesn't engage in battles with parts, so there is probably a part that is polarized with the "destructive" part.

  Example: A part of you is angry at the amount of work you are being given and wants to tell your boss off. You think you are coming from Self as you try to stop it. Whatever you say seems to solidify or inflame the Angry Part. You might find that you are blended with a Scared or Good Girl Part instead of being in Self.

Steps in Working with Polarizations

1. Recognize polarized parts

Sample:

	Part A	Part B
Name of Part	*Taskmaster*	*Procrastinator*
How does it feel in your body?	Energized, focused, tingly arms and belly	Tense, withdrawn, tired
What does it look like?	Snowplow pushing forward	Child with weights on its ankles
What does it say?	Let's go! Get a move on! You have a lot to do. Better get cracking! There's no time to waste.	It will be easier to do that later. Don't put pressure on yourself. You have to be sure it's the right thing to do. What if you can't do it? Or don't really want to do it?

2. Unblend from each part to be in Self

You can hold both parts in awareness or see them in front of you. It can also be helpful to sit with your hands resting on your thighs, palms up. Imagine that you're putting one side of the polarization in each hand. Take a few deep breaths into your belly and find the place inside of you that is neither of the parts—just you.

As in Chapter 5, unblend from each part. Let it know you are interested in getting to know it and ask it to give you some space. Check to see if any Concerned Parts are in the way.

Sample:

	Taskmaster	*Procrastinator*
Willing to unblend?	Yes	No
Concerns about unblending	No	Fear it will lose its power
Concerned Parts that show up		Fear of being pushed around

3. Clarify each part's role, positive intent, and conflict with the other part

Work with one part at a time using Steps P2–P5. Follow the procedure described in Chapter 7 for getting to know a Protector. As you are getting to know the part, find out how it feels toward the Polarized Part and perhaps any history that it holds.

While you're getting to know Part A, Part B may jump in and disrupt the process if it feels threatened. When this happens, do the negotiation again and see if it will trust you enough to let you continue. If not, you may have to work with Part B first.

Sample:

	Taskmaster	*Procrastinator*
Role in your system	To keep moving forward and accomplishing goals. To get things done. To try new things.	To avoid uncomfortable feelings, taking risks, exposure, danger, and growth
Positive intention for you	To be recognized, to feel competent, accomplished, self-satisfied, and proud. To be out there in the world and succeed.	To not be overwhelmed. To be at ease and secure.
Conflict with the other part	The Procrastinator is always getting in my way. It fogs me over and makes me tired and forgetful. It makes everything more difficult.	The Taskmaster keeps hounding me. I'm trying to relax and take my time. It's always pushing me to do things I'm afraid of and don't want to do.
Fear	We will never get to do anything or try anything new. I won't get to live my life. I won't accomplish anything and won't be recognized.	I don't want to be exposed to anything dangerous or threatening. I'm afraid of being abandoned, hurt, or rejected.

4. Develop a trusting relationship with each part

As in Chapter 6, work with each part so it feels you in Self and becomes willing to work with you. Let the part know that you understand why it does what it does and that you appreciate its efforts on your behalf. Work on any distrust that is there.

Sample:

	Taskmaster	*Procrastinator*
What the part needs from Self in order to feel trust	To know that it is heard and that its goals are valued and important	To be patient and understand its concerns

5. Decide whether to work on an Exile or depolarization

Once you have connected with each Polarized Part, you'll need to decide which way to proceed before depolarizing the situation and promoting cooperation between the parts. There are two choices:

a. Unburden the Exile(s) being protected by one part or both parts. Follow the process described in Chapters 11–17 to work with the Exile(s).

b. Facilitate a depolarization dialogue between the two parts.

Sample:

	Taskmaster	*Procrastinator*
Is the part ready for a depolarization dialogue?	Yes	No
If not, does it want to work with the protected Exile?		Yes
Exile being protected		Shamed Child

6. Get permission from each part to have a depolarization dialogue with the other under the guidance of Self

Ask each part individually if it would be willing to have a dialogue with the other part in order to resolve the conflict. If either part isn't willing, ask what it is afraid will happen in the dialogue, and reassure it that you won't let anything destructive occur. Often one part is afraid that the other part will attack it or take you over and do dangerous things. Explain that you will stay in Self and not let the other part take over or attack.

Setting up a Depolarization Dialogue

Dialogues can take place:

1. **Internally:** You stay in Self and visualize or listen to the parts talking. You might focus on alternate hands as each part speaks.

2. **Externally:** You could set up pillows or chairs to represent the parts and shift your seat or just your external focus as each part speaks out loud.

3. **Mixed:** You set up the external environment and move from chair to chair, feeling what is currently present for each part, without speaking out loud.

7. Each part states its position and then responds to the other

First, allow the Polarized Parts to stake out their conflicting positions, even though this isn't yet real dialogue, because this will give you a clear understanding of the polarization and how each part is reacting and countering the other one. However, don't allow them to attack each other. Once they have each made their points, you can move on to facilitating a dialogue between them.

Once the two Polarized Parts have begun a dialogue by stating their positions, ask each of them to say what their positive intent is for you and what they are trying to protect, if they haven't already. This begins to move the conversation beyond simply taking positions.

Sample:

	Taskmaster	*Procrastinator*
Basic position	I want to move my life forward, accomplish things that I feel are valuable, and experiment with new things that fulfill my life.	I want to feel safe and avoid being pushed into situations that make me anxious or put me at risk of failure or embarrassment.
Response	Your fears hold me back from trying new things, and I get frustrated and angry with you. I get excited about something, and you get in the way.	I have been protecting a child that was shamed. We now have done some healing work with her, and she is safer. But I have to trust that you will consider my concerns and not just run headlong into potentially uncomfortable situations or take on too much.

8. Each part listens to the other and responds accordingly (true dialogue)

Then ask each part to actually listen to what the other part is saying before responding the next time. You might even ask each one to acknowledge what the other part is saying. Then ask them to respond in a way that takes into account what is important to the other part. They don't have to agree—just to listen and respond accordingly. This begins real dialogue. It also begins to access the Self within each part or, you could say, the healthy aspect of the part. If appropriate, you can ask each part to suggest a solution that takes into account the other part's concerns and needs.

Sample:

	Taskmaster	*Procrastinator*
Note shifts in thinking as the dialogue continues	I'm glad you've worked with the Child Part. I'm willing to consult with you if you'll be reasonable about making decisions.	I want to feel safe and avoid being pushed into situations that make me anxious or put me at risk of failure or embarrassment.

9. Resolution of the polarization

Resolving the polarization can take two different forms. Often the two parts are disagreeing over a specific action they each want you to take. One level of resolution is deciding what to do. However, there is a deeper and more important kind of resolution that involves the two parts learning to appreciate each other and cooperate with each other. This will have a larger impact because it will influence future decisions and feelings that have to do with the split between these parts.

Resolutions of either kind can occur at any step in the process. Sometimes just getting to know the two parts from Self will produce a resolution. Sometimes the very beginning of the dialogue will do that. At other times, you'll get this far in the dialogue and there will still be no solution. In this case, you can step in as Self to help find a solution. If you are doing the dialogue externally, switch to a third chair or pillow that represents Self. If you are doing it internally, just speak from the place of Self.

From Self, especially after you observe the dialogue, you can sometimes see a resolution that would be agreeable to both parts that they can't see. You can offer this solution and see if they will both agree to it. Even if they don't immediately agree, intervening in this way can shift the dialogue in a fruitful direction. You can also negotiate with each part to see if it will relax its extreme stance on the condition that you will get the other part to agree to relax its extreme stance as well. This can lead to a resolution.

Sample:

	Taskmaster	*Procrastinator*
Resolution	I want you to appreciate that I want us to grow and have a fuller life. We are big now and supported, and we can use our gifts in many exciting ways. I appreciate the childlike joy that you bring, and I want to work with you.	I feel your support and appreciate that you are more connected to the outside world and have a larger vision for us. Thank you for agreeing to consult with me. I'll try to share in your excitement and believe in the resources we have today.

EXERCISE   Exploring a Polarization

Choose a polarization that you are interested in exploring. As you follow the steps below, use the information above as a reference.

1. Recognize polarized parts

Take some time to check in on the situation you are curious about. Make sure that the parts in question are really polarized. Do they hold some charged energy toward each other? Take some time to shift back and forth between the parts, noting the following information.

	Part A	Part B
Name of Part		
How does it feel in your body?		
What does it look like?		
What does it say?		

2. Unblend from each part to be in Self

Let both parts know that you want to understand them and explore the relationship between them. See if they are willing to unblend to allow this to happen. Remember that you can do Steps P2–P5 (see Appendix A, pages 155–156) for one part before moving on to the other.

	Part A	Part B
Willing to unblend?		
Concerns about unblending		
Concerned Parts that show up		

3. Clarify each part's role, positive intent, and conflict with the other part

	Part A	Part B
Role in your system		
Positive intention for you		
Conflict with the other part		
Fear		

4. Develop a trusting relationship with each part

	Part A	Part B
What the part needs from Self in order to feel trust		

5. Decide whether to work on an Exile or depolarization

If Exile work is needed first, follow the steps to work with the Exile (see Appendix A, pages 157–159) for one or both parts, remembering that they could be protecting the same Exile.

	Part A	Part B
Is the part ready for a depolarization dialogue?		
If not, does it want to work with the protected Exile?		
Exile being protected		

6. Get permission from each part to have a depolarization dialogue with the other under the guidance of Self

Check again to see if parts are ready for a depolarization dialogue.

	Part A	Part B
Is the part ready for a depolarization dialogue?		
If not, why not?		

7. Each part states its position and then responds to the other

	Part A	Part B
Basic position		
Response		

8. Each part listens to the other and responds accordingly (true dialogue)

	Part A	Part B
Note shifts in thinking as the dialogue continues		

9. Resolution of the polarization

	Part A	Part B
Resolution		

Downloadable exercise pages that accompany this workbook are available at http://personal-growth-programs.com/self-therapy-workbook-bonnie-weiss/

Appendix A

HELP SHEETS

Concerned Parts and Protectors

You can refer to this summary while you are working on yourself to guide your steps. It can also be used when you are partnering with someone.

Step 1. Getting to Know a Protector

P1. Accessing a Part

- If the part is not activated, imagine yourself in a recent situation when the part was activated.
- Sense the part in your body or get an image of the part.

P2. Unblending from a Target Part

- Check to see if you are charged up with the part's feelings.
- Check to see if you are caught up in the part's beliefs.
- If you are blended with the Target Part, options for unblending:
  - ➢ Ask the part to separate from you so you can get to know it.
  - ➢ Move back to separate from the part.
  - ➢ Get an image of the part at a distance from you.
  - ➢ Do a short centering/grounding meditation. Draw the part.
- If the part doesn't separate, ask what it is afraid would happen if it did separate.
- Explain to the part the value of separating or reassure it about its fears.

P3. Checking for Self-Leadership and Unblending from a Concerned Part

- Check to see how you feel toward the Target Part right now.
- If you feel compassionate, curious, and so on, you are in Self. Move on to P4.

- If you don't, unblend the Concerned Part:
  - ➤ Ask the Concerned Part if it would be willing to step aside (or relax) just for now so you can get to know the Target Part from an open place.
  - ➤ If it is willing, check again to see how you feel toward the Target Part, and repeat.
  - ➤ If it isn't willing to step aside, explain to it the value of stepping aside.
  - ➤ If it still won't, ask what it is afraid would happen if it did and reassure it about its fears.
  - ➤ If it still won't, make the Concerned Part the Target Part and work with it.

P4. Getting to Know a Protector

- Invite the part to tell you about itself.
- The part may answer in words, images, body sensations, emotions, or direct knowing.
  - ➤ What do you do? What is your role?
  - ➤ What do you feel? What makes you feel so (feeling)?
  - ➤ How do you relate to people? How do you interact with other parts?
  - ➤ How do you feel about (external event or feeling)?
  - ➤ How long have you been doing (your role)?
  - ➤ What do you want for us? What do you hope to accomplish by (doing your role)?
  - ➤ What are you afraid would happen if you didn't (do your role)? (This moves toward an Exile that the part is protecting.)

P5. Developing a Trusting Relationship with a Protector

- You can foster trust by saying the following to the Protector (if true).
  - ➤ I understand why you (do your role).
  - ➤ I appreciate your efforts on my behalf.

Exiles

You can refer to this summary while you are working on yourself to guide your steps. It can also be used when you are partnering with someone.

Step 2. Getting Permission to Work with an Exile

- If necessary, ask the Protector to show you the Exile.
- Ask its permission to get to know the Exile.
- If it won't give permission, ask what it is afraid would happen if you accessed the Exile.
  - ➤ The Exile has too much pain. Explain that you will stay in Self and get to know the Exile, not dive into its pain.
  - ➤ There isn't any point in going into the pain. Explain that you can heal the Exile.
  - ➤ The Protector will have no role and will therefore be eliminated. Explain that the Protector can choose a new role in your psyche.

Step 3. Getting to Know an Exile

E1. Accessing an Exile

- Sense it in your body or get an image of it.

E2. Unblending from an Exile

- If you are blended with an Exile:
  - ➤ Ask the Exile to contain its feelings so you can be there for it.
  - ➤ Consciously separate from the Exile and return to Self.
  - ➤ Get an image of the Exile at a distance from you.
  - ➤ Do a centering/grounding induction.
- If the Exile won't contain its feelings:
  - ➤ Ask what it is afraid would happen if it did.
  - ➤ Explain: You really want to witness its feelings and story, but you need to be separate to do that.
  - ➤ Conscious blending: If you can tolerate it, it is OK to feel the Exile's pain.

E3. Unblending from Concerned Parts

- Check how you feel toward the Exile.
- If you aren't in Self or don't feel compassion, unblend any Concerned Parts.
- They are usually afraid of your getting overwhelmed by the Exile's pain or the Exile taking over.
- Explain that you will stay in Self and not give the Exile power.

E4. Finding Out About an Exile

- Ask: What do you feel? What makes you feel so (feeling)?

E5. Developing a Trusting Relationship with an Exile

- Let the Exile know that you want to hear its story.
- Communicate to the Exile that you feel compassion, caring, etc., toward it.
- Check to see if the Exile can sense you there and how it is responding to your compassion.

Step 4. Accessing and Witnessing Childhood Origins

- Ask the Exile to show you an image or memory of when it learned to feel this way in childhood.
- Ask the Exile how this made it feel.
- Check to make sure the Exile has shown you everything it wants witnessed.
- After witnessing, check to see if the Exile believes that you understand how bad it was.

Step 5. Reparenting an Exile

- Bring yourself (as Self) into the childhood situation and ask the Exile what it needs from you to heal it or change what happened. Give that to the Exile through your internal imagination.
- Check to see how the Exile is responding to your reparenting.
- If it can't sense you or isn't taking in your caring, ask why and work with that.

Step 6. Retrieving an Exile

- One of the things the Exile may need is to be taken out of the childhood situation.
- You can bring it into some place in the present, into your body, or into an imaginary place. Let it tell you where it wants to be taken.

Step 7. Unburdening an Exile

- Identify the burden the Exile is carrying—an extreme feeling or belief.
- Ask the Exile if it wants to give up or release the burden and if it feels ready to do so.
- If it doesn't want to, ask what it is afraid would happen if it let the burden go. Then handle those fears.
- How does the Exile carry the burden in or on its body?
- Ask what the Exile would like to release the burden to: light, water, wind, earth, fire, or anything else.
- Once the burden is gone, notice what positive qualities or feelings arise in the Exile or what positive qualities it would like to take in.

Step 8. Integration and Unburdening a Protector

- Introduce the transformed Exile to the Protector.
- See if the Protector now realizes that its role of protection is no longer necessary.
- If necessary, take it through an unburdening and notice what positive qualities arise.
- The Protector can choose a new role in your psyche.
- Imagine yourself at the original trailhead and see if any parts get activated.

MEDITATIONS

These are the transcripts for the three MP3 meditations that accompany this book.

Meditation Transcript: Getting into Self

Take a moment to quiet yourself and go inside.

Sit up straight. Become aware of your breathing, and gradually deepen your breath.

Wiggle your body a bit until it settles down.

Feel the weight of your legs and let them relax,

Feel the weight of your arms and let them relax,

Let your shoulders be heavy and your jaw slacken.

Breathing in cool white mist and breathing out gray fog may help you relax and become still.

Breathe in white mist. Breathe out gray fog.

In and out.

In and out.

The following Rumi poem is very powerful when read out loud.

THE GUEST HOUSE

by Jelaluddin Rumi, translation by Coleman Barks

This being human is a guest house.
Every morning a new arrival.
A joy, a depression, a meanness,
some momentary awareness comes
as an unexpected visitor.
Welcome and entertain them all!
Even if they are a crowd of sorrows,

who violently sweep your house
empty of its furniture,
still, treat each guest honorably.
He may be clearing you out
for some new delight.
The dark thought, the shame, the malice.
meet them at the door laughing and invite them in.
Be grateful for whatever comes.
because each has been sent
as a guide from beyond.

Now take a moment and see who the guests are in your house.
Notice them one by one as they make themselves known to you.
You may recognize them as a thought ... a feeling ... a sensation in or around your body ... a distraction ... a memory ...

As you invite each of them in, give them a seat at some sort of table or circle. It could be an intimate kitchen table or a large dining room table, a conference table, a campfire, or anything else.

Place yourself at the head of this table so that you can make contact with each of your guests as they take a seat. Welcome them here. They are all welcome, big or small, feisty or sullen, clear or shadowy. See how it feels for you to be at the head of this table, acknowledging them all.

When you are ready, gradually bring yourself back to the room.

Meditation Transcript: Appreciating Protectors

Close your eyes and go inside. Begin by paying attention to your body's sensations. Notice the sensations that you are aware of in this moment and be present with them. Feel what is going on in your belly and just relax into your body in this moment.

Now become aware of some of the Protectors you have worked with. Take a moment to notice how each of them is trying to help you. Even if its impact is negative, each Protector is trying to keep you from feeling pain or keep an Exile from being harmed. Each one has a positive intent for you. Notice what the positive intent is from each of your Protectors.

Be aware that your Protectors have been working for many years to protect you. Many of them have been working very hard for most of your life.

Some of them think that what they are doing is vitally necessary to keep you from pain or from being thrown into chaos. Other Protectors think that their jobs are vitally necessary to keep you from being judged, controlled, attacked, or abandoned. They may not even like their job, but they believe that somebody has to do it. Even if their efforts backfire or cause serious problems for you, their hearts are in the right place, and they want the best for you.

Take a moment to appreciate your Protectors and their hard work on your behalf. Parts of you may have been judgmental of them and may have wished that they would go away. But now appreciate their efforts to help you and guard you. Also feel your compassion for them because of their desperate need to avoid pain.

Let your Protectors know that you understand what they have been trying to do for you and that you appreciate their efforts, and open your heart to them. Notice how they are responding to you. Check in and notice what you are feeling right now.

Now gradually, slowly bring yourself back to the room.

Meditation Transcript: Soothing a Triggered Exile

Pause for a moment and take a journey inside.

Begin by finding a safe, comfortable place to sit or lie down

where your back can be straight and your breath can move freely.

Now bring your attention to your breath.

As you become aware of your breath, notice whether it is fast or slow.

Is it high in your chest or lower down in your belly?

On your next inhalation, see if you can bring the breath farther down into your body,

    opening your abdomen.

Breathe in and out.

A breath pattern that is helpful in calming yourself is a sequence of breaths:

    Breathe in for two beats,

    Hold your breath for two beats,

    Breathe out for two beats,

    Stay empty for two beats.

Close your eyes and try this sequence of breaths three times.

As you get more comfortable with this pattern, you can increase the number of beats

    that you hold the breath.

Now take a moment to check your body and notice what you are aware of.

    Where are you tense?

    Where are you open?

    Where is there contraction or pain?

    Where is there fluttering or energy moving freely?

Bring your breath to any area that needs attention.

You might want to place your hand on an area of your body

    that needs attention or support.

Often these body sensations can be the result of having emotions triggered.

We can see them as holding or representing younger parts of ourselves

    that may have been activated recently.

There may be memories surfacing that need some attention or soothing.

Keep your breathing steady as you allow whatever needs to surface

    to do so in its own time.

Keep your feet grounded, your shoulders and jaw relaxed.

You may have a sense of a Child Part that is holding some pain from the past.

Remember that you are here in your life now with more capacity and strength

    than when you were young.

You have the capacity for compassion and support.

There is greater distance and deeper wisdom.

You can offer this to the Child Parts as they arise.

See what these Child Parts need from you.

    Do they need to be listened to?

    Do they need to be rescued?

    Do they need to be held?

Check to see how you are feeling about providing these things for the Child Parts

    and do whatever you can.

You might place your hand on your heart and breathe a few breaths into your heart,

    enlivening it and opening it.

Breathe in and out.

Allow one Child Part to come forward who especially needs your caring attention

    right now.

What would it be like to be the compassionate, nurturing parent

    that this wounded Inner Child needs right now?

Can you listen to his or her pain with caring?

If it is appropriate, imagine holding this child in your arms.

Let it know that you are here for him or her.

Give this Inner Child the love that he or she needs

and whatever else is appropriate—acceptance, validation, encouragement, support,

    appreciation.

Let yourself be with this child as long as it feels right to do so.

You may offer to bring him or her out of the past and into the present,
    or to some other safe place where you know he or she will be protected.
Feel yourself doing that now.

When the child is settled and comfortable,
Wiggle your fingers and toes, and gradually come back to the room.

Appendix C

DEFINITIONS OF TERMS

Accessing a Part. Tuning in to a part experientially through an image, emotion, body sensation, or internal dialogue so you can work with the part using IFS.

Activation of a Part. When a part becomes triggered by a situation or a person so that it influences your feelings and actions.

Active Listening. When you are the witness for someone doing an IFS session, and you attempt to understand their experience and reflect that back to them.

Blending. The situation in which a part has taken over your consciousness so that you feel its feelings, believe its attitudes are true, and act according to its impulses. Blending is a more extreme form of activation.

Burden. A painful emotion or negative belief about yourself or the world that a part has taken on as the result of a past harmful situation or relationship, usually from childhood.

Childhood Origin. An incident or relationship from childhood that produced enough pain or trauma that it caused an Exile to take on a burden.

Concerned Part. A part that feels judgmental or angry toward the Target Part. When you are blended with a Concerned Part, you aren't in Self.

Conscious Blending. The situation in which you choose to feel a part's emotions because doing so will be helpful in the IFS process. You are aware that you are blended and can un-blend easily if necessary.

Exile. A young child part that is carrying pain from the past.

Extreme Role. A role that is dysfunctional or problematic because the part carries a burden from the past or because a Protector is trying to protect an Exile. An extreme part is a part that has an extreme role.

Firefighter. A type of Protector that impulsively jumps in when the pain of an Exile is starting to come up in order to distract you from the pain or numb it.

Healthy Role. A role that is the natural function of a part when it has no burdens. A healthy part is a part that has a healthy role.

Implicit Memory. A childhood memory that shows up as a vague body sensation or a fragmented image, giving you only a partial sense of the actual incident or relationship.

Manager. A Protector that tries to proactively arrange your life and your psyche so that the pain of Exiles does not come to the surface.

Part. A subpersonality, which has its own feelings, perceptions, beliefs, motivations, and memories.

Polarization. A situation in which two parts are in conflict about how you should act or feel.

Positive Intent. The underlying positive motivation of each part. The role it plays is an attempt to help you or protect you, even if the effect of the role is negative.

Protector. A part that tries to block off pain that is arising inside you or protect you from hurtful incidents or distressing relationships in your current life.

Reparenting. The step in the IFS process in which the Self gives an Exile what it needs to feel better or change a harmful childhood situation.

Retrieval. The step in the IFS process in which the Self takes an Exile out of a harmful childhood situation and into a place where it can be safe and comfortable.

Role. The job that a part performs to help you. It may be primarily internal, or it may involve the way the part interacts with people and acts in the world.

Seat of Consciousness. The place in the psyche that determines your identity, choices, feelings, and perceptions. The Self is the natural occupant of the seat of consciousness, though parts can take over the seat by blending.

Self. The core aspect of you that is your true self and your spiritual center. The Self is relaxed, open, and accepting of yourself and others. It is curious, compassionate, calm, and interested in connecting with other people and with your parts.

Self-Leadership. The situation in which your parts trust you, in Self, to make decisions and take action in your life.

Target Part. The part you are focusing on to work with at the moment.

Trailhead. A psychological issue that involves one or more parts. Following it can lead to healing.

Unblending. Separating from a part that is blended with you so that you are in Self.

Unburdening. The step in the IFS process in which the Self helps an Exile to release its burdens through an internal ritual.

Witnessing. The step in the IFS process in which the Self witnesses the childhood origin of a part's burdens.

Appendix D
RESOURCES

Finding an IFS Therapist: The website of the Center for Self Leadership, the official IFS organization, contains a geographic listing of IFS-certified therapists and practitioners. Many offer IFS sessions by telephone. www.selfleadership.org

IFS Telecourses. Basic IFS, Exiles, Inner Critic, and Beyond Eating telecourses for the general public. Visit www.personal-growth-programs.com or email us: bonnieweiss@gmail.com or earley.jay@gmail.com

Inner Critic Questionnaire and Profiling Program for your Inner Critic and Inner Champion is available at www.psychemaps.com or www.personal-growth-programs.com.

Books

Self-Therapy: A Step-by-Step Guide to Creating Wholeness and Healing Your Inner Child Using IFS, by Jay Earley. Shows how to do IFS sessions on your own or with a partner. Also a manual of the IFS method that can be used by therapists.

Freedom From Your Inner Critic: A Self-Therapy Approach, by Jay Earley and Bonnie Weiss. Also, a companion workbook can be downloaded free from our website www.personal-growth-programs.com.

Illustrated Workbook for Freedom for Your Inner Critic, by Bonnie Weiss. A good resource for clients or classes with adolescents new to the concept of parts and the Inner Critic.

Activating Your Inner Champion Instead of Your Inner Critic, by Jay Earley and Bonnie Weiss, describes the seven types of Inner Critics and allows you to profile your version of them in detail using a web program. Each of the seven has an Inner Champion that is the magic bullet for transforming that particular type of Critic.

The Pattern System, by Jay Earley. The Pattern System is a systematic approach to understanding personality that can lead directly to psychological healing and personal growth. This book provides an overview of the system for helping professionals, psychologists, and the general public.

Pattern Books. We have published five books that deal with specific patterns from the Pattern System. Each book is connected to a workbook on the web that allows you to actively work with the pattern and develop a practice for changing it and manifesting the healthy capacity in your life. The books are: *Embracing Intimacy, Taking Action* (Procrastination), *Letting Go of Perfectionism, Beyond Caretaking,* and *A Pleaser No Longer.*

Introduction to the Internal Family Systems Model, by Richard Schwartz. A basic introduction to parts and IFS for clients and potential clients.

Internal Family Systems Therapy, by Richard Schwartz. The primary professional book on IFS and a must-read for therapists.

The Mosaic Mind: Empowering the Tormented Selves of Child Abuse Survivors, by Richard Schwartz and Regina Goulding. A professional book on using IFS with trauma, especially sexual abuse.

You Are the One You've Been Waiting For: Bringing Courageous Love to Intimate Relationships, by Richard Schwartz. A popular book providing an IFS perspective on intimate relationships.

Self-Therapy Card Deck, produced by Bonnie Weiss. The IFS process using illustrations from *Self-Therapy*.

Audio Products

Meditations: We have produced meditations for each of the steps of the IFS process and meditations to help evoke the Inner Champions for all of the Inner Critics. http://www.personal-growth-programs.com/store/meditations

Demonstration Sessions: A good selection of demonstration sessions by Bonnie Weiss and Jay Earley. There are demonstrations of each step of the IFS process and full sessions showing how the IFS process is experienced by real clients. Also include work on each of the Inner Critics. http://www.personal-growth-programs.com/store/demonstration-sessions

Web-Based Resources

Self-Therapy Journey, by Jay Earley. A web application for personal growth and psychological healing based on the Pattern System and IFS. It includes descriptions of psychological issues, stories, checklists, guided journaling, guided meditations, customized reports, and homework practices.

Downloadable exercise pages that accompany this workbook are available at http://personal-growth-programs.com/self-therapy-workbook-bonnie-weiss/

Made in the USA
Lexington, KY
20 July 2016